AMSTERDAM

CONTENTS

EXPERIENCE

NEED TO KNOW

Left: Montelbaanstoren seen from the Singel
Right: People picnicking in Sarphatipark

Main Contributors Robin Gauldie,
Robin Pascoe, Christopher Catling

Design Nidhi Mehra, Priyanka Thakur

Editorial Rachel Fox, Shikha Kulkarni, Beverly
Smart, Hollie Teague

Indexer Nayan Keshan

Picture Research Sumita Khatwani, Ellen Root

Cartography Suresh Kumar, Casper Morris

Jacket Designers Maxine Pedliham, Amy Cox

DTP Jason Little, Rohit Rojal

Delhi Team Head Malavika Talukder

Art Director Maxine Pedliham

Publishing Director Georgina Dee

Conceived by Priyanka Thakur
and Shikha Kulkarni

Printed and bound in China

Content previously published in DK Eyewitness
Amsterdam (2019). This abridged edition first
published in 2020
Published in Great Britain by
Dorling Kindersley Limited
80 Strand, London WC2R 0RL

Published in the United States by DK Publishing,
1450 Broadway, Suite 801, New York, NY 10018

19 20 21 22 10 9 8 7 6 5 4 3 2 1

**The information in this DK Eyewitness
Travel Guide is checked regularly.**
Every effort has been made to ensure this book
is up-to-date at the time of going to press.
However, details such as addresses, opening
hours, prices and travel information, are liable to
change. The publishers cannot accept
responsibility for any consequences arising
from the use of this book, nor for any
material on third-party websites. If you
have any comments, please write to: DK
Eyewitness Travel Guides, Dorling Kindersley,
80 Strand, London WC2R 0RL, UK, or email:
travelguides@dk.com.

KEY TO MAIN ICONS

📍	Map	🚤	Canalbus
🏠	Address/Location	⛴	Ferry
☎	Telephone	ℹ	Visitor information
🚆	Train	🕐	Open
Ⓜ	Metro	🚫	Closed
🚋	Tram	🌐	Website
🚌	Bus		

MIX
Paper from
responsible sources
FSC™ C018179
www.fsc.org

WELCOME TO
AMSTERDAM

With its reflective waterways, tilting canal houses and humpback bridges, Amsterdam is undeniably picturesque. But this city contains multitudes: museums and street art, cruises and cycle rides, Dutch cuisine and world street food. Whatever your ideal break to Amsterdam includes, this DK Eyewitness Mini Map and Guide is the perfect travel companion.

Amsterdam is a city where both the past and the present are keenly felt. Majestic 17th-century mansions are perfectly preserved, while 20th-century warehouses have been transformed into quirky entertainment complexes. The vast Rijksmuseum, with its Old Masters, sits beside the Stedelijk Museum, which displays puzzling contemporary art installations. Infamously hedonistic, the city's nightlife encompasses so much more than the Red Light District. As well as relentless nightclubs, there are first-class concert venues, including the innovative Muziekgebouw aan 't IJ.

Beyond Amsterdam, postcard-pretty villages and heritage-rich cities are never far away. Windswept beaches, flat, windmill-dotted fields and striped bulbfields punctuate the Dutch landscape. The cities have plenty to offer too. There's ultramodern Rotterdam and historic Haarlem, stately Den Haag and laid-back Leiden. World-class museums await, including the Mauritshuis and Utrecht's museum of Miffy – the little white rabbit.

With so many different things to discover and experience, Amsterdam can seem overwhelming. We've broken the city down into easily navigable chapters, highlighting each area's unmissable sights and unexpected delights. Add insider tips, leisurely walks, a comprehensive fold-out map and a need-to-know section full of expert advice for before and during your trip, and you've got an indispensable guidebook. Enjoy the book, and enjoy Amsterdam.

↓ Amsterdam's skyline at sunset

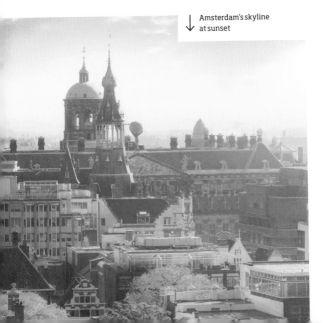

NIEUWE ZIJDE

Crammed with hotels, shops, bars and restaurants, this is Amsterdam's busiest tourist district. At its centre, Dam Square bustles with visitors heading to the sights as street performers clamour to grab their attention. Enclaves like the serene Begijnhof provide a refuge from the "New Side's" relentless commercialism.

Munttoren and a canal-side restaurant at dusk ↓

↑ Exhibits from the 20th century on display in Amsterdam DNA

AMSTERDAM MUSEUM

📍 E5 🏠 Kalverstraat 92, St Luciensteeg 27 🚊 2, 4, 11, 12, 14, 24 Ⓜ Rokin
🕙 10am–5pm daily 🗓 27 April, 25 Dec 🌐 amsterdammuseum.nl

The city's historical museum explores Amsterdam's dramatic evolution from marshland to modern times, as well as the city's future. The setting tells a story just as varied as the one told by the main collection. The red-brick building began life as the Convent of St Lucien, before it was turned into a civic orphanage two years after the Alteration.

At the museum's heart is the Amsterdam DNA exhibition, which offers a multimedia introduction to the development of Amsterdam, from its humble origins as a small fishing village at the mouth of the Amstel in the Middle Ages to today's cosmopolitan city. Visitors can then explore the other rooms, where aspects of Amsterdam's history are dealt with in more detail, including the city's Golden Age in the 17th century. The Amsterdam Gallery also covers both the past and the present with exhibits ranging from 16th-century portraits to modern-day graffiti. Meanwhile, the Regents' Chamber and The Little Orphanage unlock the building's history.

↑ The globe, crafted by Willem Blaeu (cartographer of the Dutch East India Company), on display in Amsterdam DNA

NIEUWE KERK

📍F4 🏠Dam Square 🚋2, 4, 11, 12, 13, 14, 17, 24 🕐10am–5pm daily (during exhibitions only; check website) 🌐nieuwekerk.nl

The medieval "New Church" is both stately and surprising, hosting not only royal coronations but also impressive exhibitions on inspiring individuals, different cultures, contemporary art and photography.

Dating from the 14th century, Amsterdam's second parish church was built as the population outgrew the Oude Kerk. During its turbulent history, the church was destroyed several times by fire, rebuilt and then stripped of its finery after the Alteration. It reached its present size in the 1650s. Highlights of the interior include the Great Organ (1645), which is adorned with marbled-wood cherubs and has shutters painted by Jacob van Campen, Rombout Verhulst's tomb of Michiel de Ruyter (1607–76) – the heroic admiral who died in battle against the French at Messina – and the carved pulpit (1664). Since 1814, all the Dutch monarchs have been crowned here.

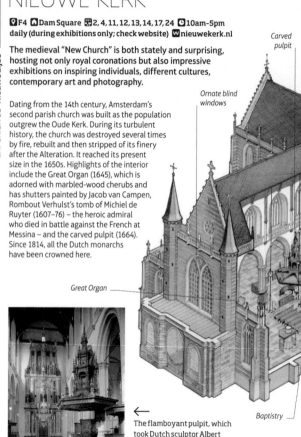

Carved pulpit

Ornate blind windows

Great Organ

Baptistry

← The flamboyant pulpit, which took Dutch sculptor Albert Vinckenbrinck 15 years to carve

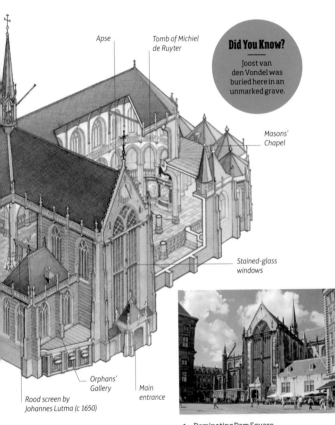

Apse

Tomb of Michiel de Ruyter

Did You Know?

Joost van den Vondel was buried here in an unmarked grave.

Masons' Chapel

Stained-glass windows

Orphans' Gallery

Main entrance

Rood screen by Johannes Lutma (c 1650)

↑ The Nieuwe Kerk's magnificent interior

↑ Dominating Dam Square, the church, with its huge stained-glass windows

MUSEUM ONS' LIEVE HEER OP SOLDER

📍G4 🏠Oudezijds Voorburgwal 38 🚊4, 14, 24
🕐10am–6pm Mon–Sat, 1–6pm Sun and public hols
📅27 Apr 🌐opsolder.nl

Did You Know?

The church is painted *caput mortuum*, or "dead head" pink.

Tucked away on the edge of the Red Light District is a restored 17th-century canal house, with two smaller houses to the rear. The upper storeys conceal a secret Catholic church known as Our Lord in the Attic (Ons' Lieve Heer op Solder).

Our Lord in the Attic

After the Alteration, when Amsterdam officially became Protestant, many hidden churches were built throughout the city. Bourgeois merchant Jan Hartman added this chapel to his house in 1663. It was extended in around 1735 to create more seating space.

The building became a museum in 1888, and displays fine church silver, religious artifacts and paintings. Next door to the church is an exhibition space, café and shop.

Simple spout gable on the first house

Canal room

Main entrance

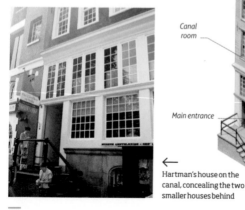

← Hartman's house on the canal, concealing the two smaller houses behind

Wooden viewing gallery of the church

Our Lord in the Attic served the Catholic community until Sint Nicolaasbasiliek was finished in 1887.

Sacristy, where vestments were kept

The landing where the tiny wooden confessional stands was the living room of the rear house.

The 17th-century kitchen was originally part of the priest's living quarters.

← The three houses that make up the Museum Ons' Lieve Heer Op Solder

The parlour

A chaplain's tiny box bedroom is hidden off a bend in the stairs. There was a resident chaplain in the church from 1663.

↑ The canal room is where 17th-century residents would have spent the day.

BEGIJNHOF

📍 E5 🏠 Spui (entrance at Gedempte Begijnensloot)
🚋 2, 4, 11, 12, 14, 24 🕐 Gates: 9am–5pm daily

With its beautiful rows of houses overlooking a well-kept green, the Begijnhof is the perfect place for some respite from the frenetic energy of the Nieuwe Zijde.

The Begijnhof was originally built in 1346 as a sanctuary for the Begijntjes, a lay Catholic sisterhood who lived like nuns, although they took no monastic vows. In return for lodgings within the complex, these worthy women undertook to educate the poor and care for the city's sick. Nothing survives of the earliest dwellings, but the Begijnhof still retains a sanctified atmosphere. No groups are allowed and visitors should respect the residents' privacy.

↑ The Engelse Kerk's stark interior reflects its Presbyterian past

Het Houten Huis

The Begijnhof Chapel, a clandestine church (Nos 29–30), was completed in 1680.

Spui entrance

↑ A statue of Jesus stands in the middle of Begijnhof's green

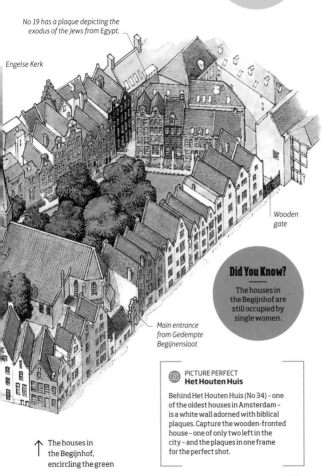

No 19 has a plaque depicting the exodus of the Jews from Egypt.

Engelse Kerk

Wooden gate

Did You Know?

The houses in the Begijnhof are still occupied by single women.

Main entrance from Gedempte Begijnensloot

PICTURE PERFECT
Het Houten Huis

Behind Het Houten Huis (No 34) - one of the oldest houses in Amsterdam - is a white wall adorned with biblical plaques. Capture the wooden-fronted house - one of only two left in the city - and the plaques in one frame for the perfect shot.

↑ The houses in the Begijnhof, encircling the green

Retaining its former opulence, Magna Plaza's colonnaded interior

EXPERIENCE MORE

Magna Plaza

📍E4 🏛Nieuwezijds Voorburgwal 182 🚊2, 11, 12, 13, 17 🕐11am-7pm Mon, 10am-7pm Tue, Wed, Fri & Sat, 10am-9pm Thu, noon-7pm Sun 🌐magnaplaza.nl

A wall panel on the current building's façade depicts the site's original function. In 1748, it was a *postkantoor* (post office), but it was taken out of service in 1854. The present building was completed in 1899. C H Peters (1847–1932), the architect, was ridiculed for the extravagance of its Neo-Gothic design: critics dubbed the elaborately decorated exterior, with its spindly towers, "post-office Gothic". It was redeveloped in 1992, though the grand dimensions of Peters' design were beautifully preserved, and is now an elegant shop-ping mall, set over three floors, called the Magna Plaza.

Beurs van Berlage

📍F4 🏛Damrak 2 🚊4, 14, 24 🕐Only during exhibitions 🌐beursvan berlage.nl

Built in 1903 to a design by Hendrik Petrus Berlage (1856–1934), this is a striking modernist building. The former stock exchange's clean, functional appear-ance marked a departure from late 19th-century Revivalist architecture. Its curvaceous lines, plain exterior and, above all, Berlage's imaginative use of red brick as a decorative construction material inspired the later architects of the Amsterdam School. It has an impressive frieze above the entrance show-ing the evolution of man from Adam to stockbroker. The building is entered through a 40-m (130-ft) clock tower that gives access to three massive halls once used as trading floors.

Inside, the main hall is decorated with ceramic friezes depicting different labourers, including miners and coffee pickers.

Now used as a conference venue, it also hosts a variety of changing exhibitions and concerts, and there is a good bistro. Guided tours of the build-ing allow you to climb the bell tower for extensive views over Amsterdam.

Torensluis

📍E4 🏛Singel between Torensteeg and Oude Leliestraat 🚊2, 11, 12, 13, 17

The Torensluis is one of the oldest and widest bridges in Amsterdam. Spanning a width of 42 m (138 ft), it was built on the site of a 17th-century sluice gate and took its name from a tower that stood on the bridge until it was demolished in 1829 (its outline is marked in the pavement). A jail was built in its foundations and if you look carefully you can see the barred windows and arched entrance leading to the old dungeon below the water line.

The statue dominating the bridge is of the 19th-century Dutch author Eduard Douwes Dekker (1820–87), who wrote under the pseudonym Multatuli. His novel *Max Havelaar*, which was published in 1860, is a polemic against the atrocities committed by Dutch colonialists in the East Indies (modern-day Indonesia). The protagonist, Max Havelaar, battles against the corrupt government of Java. The book was a source of encouragement to reformers, but the Dutch were ultimately evicted from their empire only by force.

EAT

Visrestaurant Lucius

Lobster and crab are specialities at this long-established seafood restaurant. It has an outstanding set menu.

📍E5 🏛Spuistraat 247 🌐lucius.nl

€€€

Kam Yin City Centre

Traditional Surinamese *roti* (pancakes with either a vegetable or meat filling) are a house speciality.

📍G3 🏛Warmoes-straat 6 🌐kamyin.nl

€€€

Munttoren

📍F6 🏛Muntplein
🚋4, 14, 24 🚇Rokin
🕐Shop: Apr-Oct: 9:30am-9pm daily; Nov-Mar till 6pm

The polygonal base of the Munttoren (mint tower) was part of the Regsulierspoort – the southern gateway in Amsterdam's medieval city wall. The gate was destroyed by fire in 1618, but the base survived. In the following year, Hendrick de Keyser added the clock tower (closed to the public), capped with a steeple and openwork orb. The carillon was designed by François Hemony in 1699, and rings every 15 minutes. The tower acquired its name in 1673, during the French occupation, when the former city mint was temporarily housed here.

The ground floor is home to a shop that sells delftware still made by hand at the Royal Delft factory.

Nationaal Monument

📍F4 🏛Dam Square
🚋4, 9, 14, 16, 24

Sculpted by John Rädecker (1885–1956) and designed by architect J J P Oud (1890–1963), the 22-m (70-ft) obelisk that looms over Dam Square commemorates Dutch World War II casualties. It was unveiled in 1956, and is fronted by two lions – heraldic symbols of the Netherlands. Embedded in the wall behind are urns containing earth from all the Dutch provinces and the former colonies of Indonesia, the Antilles and Surinam.

← The Nationaal Monument dominating Dam Square

Lutherse Kerk

📍 F3 🏛 Kattengat 2
🚋 2, 11, 12, 13, 17
🚫 To the public

The Lutherse Kerk, located in Singel, was designed by Adriaan Dortsman (1625–82) and opened in 1671. It is sometimes known as the Ronde Lutherse Kerk, being the first Dutch Reformed church to feature a circular ground plan and two upper galleries, giving the whole congregation a clear view of the pulpit.

In 1882 a fire started by careless plumbers destroyed everything except the exterior walls. When the interior and entrance were rebuilt in 1883, they were made squarer and more ornate, in keeping with ecclesiastical architecture of that time. A vaulted copper dome replaced the earlier ribbed version.

Falling attendances led to the closure and deconsecration of the church in 1935 and, since 1975, it has acted as Renaissance Amsterdam Hotel's conference centre and banqueting chamber. Take time to admire its unique exterior, which stands out among the canal houses.

Sint Nicolaasbasiliek

📍 G3 🏛 Prins Hendrikkade 73 🚋 2, 11, 12, 13, 14, 17, 24 Ⓜ Centraal Station
🕐 Noon–3pm Mon & Sat, 11am–4pm Tue–Fri
🌐 nicolaas-parochie.nl

Sint Nicolaas, the patron saint of seafarers, is an important icon in Holland. Many churches are named after him, and 5 December (Sint Nicolaas Day) is the Netherlands' principal day for the giving of presents.

1,281

bridges span the 50 km (31 miles) of canals in Amsterdam.

In November, the gift-giving saint arrives at the church, accompanied by a helper, Zwarte Piet (Black Pete) in blackface make-up. This tradition in fact dates only from the 19th century, and has been denounced by anti-racism campaigners.

Amsterdam's biggest Catholic church, the Sint Nicolaasbasiliek was designed by A C Bleys (1842–1912) and completed in 1887. Despite its rather grim and forbidding exterior, with its twin towers looming over

The circular copper dome of Lutherse Kerk reflected in the canal ↓

eedijk and the Oosterdok, int Nicolaasbasiliek's completion marked the rehabilitation of the Catholic faith after centuries of clandestine worship during the period when Amsterdam was officially Protestant. The joy of the congregation is reflected in the church's interior, which is brightened by stained-glass windows set in its imposing dome.

Services are held most days (Tuesday in English), and the church occasionally hosts concerts and recitals featuring the magnificently restored 19th-century Bauer organ.

Koninklijk Paleis

☷ F4 **☐** Dam Square **☷** 2, 4, 11, 12, 13, 14, 17, 24 **☐** Check website for details **☒** paleisamster dam.nl

The Koninklijk Paleis, still used by the king for official events, was built as the Stadhuis (town hall). Work began in 1648, after the end of the Eighty Years' War with Spain. Dominating its surroundings, the Classically inspired design by Jacob van Campen (1595–1657) reflects the city's mood of confidence after the Dutch victory. Civic pride is also shown in the mythological sculptures by Artus Quellien (1609–68), which decorate the pediments, and in the carrillon

by François Hemony (1609–67). The full magnificence is best seen in the Burgerzaal (citizens' hall). Based on the assembly halls of ancient Rome, this 30-m- (95-ft-) high room boasts a marble floor inlaid with a celestial map flanked by the two terrestrial hemispheres.

Allard Pierson Museum

☷ F6 **☐** Oude Turfmarkt 127 **☷** 4, 14, 24 **Ⓜ** Rokin **☐** 10am-5pm Tue-Fri, 1-5pm Sat & Sun **☐** 1 Jan, 27 Apr, 25 Dec **☒** allard piersonmuseum.nl

Amsterdam's only specialist archaeological collection is named after Allard Pierson (1831–96), a humanist and scholar. Part of the University of Amsterdam and housed in a former bank, this museum is not just a dusty collection of ancient relics. Although small, it interestingly links vanished civilizations with the modern world through its collection of thousands of objects from the ancient worlds of Greece, Rome, Egypt and beyond. Look out for a case of rather gruesome Egyptian mummy remains and a film showing the process of mummification, a computer that enables you to write your name in hieroglyphics, a jointed Greek doll from 300 BC and some fine Roman

DRINK

Wynand Fockink

Famous *proeflokaal* with a huge choice of *jenevers* and beers.

☷ F5 **☐** Pijlsteeg 31 **☒** wynand-fockink.nl

In de Wildeman

This tavern has at least 18 craft beers on tap and 200 more by the bottle.

☷ F3 **☐** Kolksteeg 3 **☐** Sun **☒** indewildeman.nl

Café Hoppe

A 17th-century *bruin café* (local pub) serving limited-edition craft ales, traditional *jenevers* and liqueurs.

☷ E6 **☐** Spui 18 **☒** cafehoppe.com

jewellery. The Greek pottery collection has examples of black-figure and red-figure pottery produced in the 5th and 6th centuries BC. The museum also hosts challenging themed exhibitions that shed new light on European history. Located next door is Amsterdam University's special collections department.

A SHORT WALK

NIEUWE ZIJDE

Distance 1.5 km (1 mile) **Nearest metro** Rokin
Time 15 minutes

Although much of the medieval Nieuwe Zijde has disappeared, the area is still rich in buildings that relate to the city's past. A walk from Dam Square to Spui takes you past examples of architecture from the 15th to the 20th century. You'll stroll along narrow streets and alleys which follow the course of some of the earliest dykes and footpaths. Along the way, pause at traditional gabled houses that have been turned into bustling shops and cafés. Financial institutions on Rokin and Nes have made way for chic department stores and lively cafés. Nes is also known for its alternative theatre venues.

Did You Know?

Dam Square derives its name from its original function - damming the Amstel river.

Kalverstraat, a busy shopping area, took its name from the livestock market which was regularly held here during the 15th century.

Wall plaques and maps showing the walled medieval city are on display in the Amsterdam Museum – a converted 16th-century orphanage.

Two churches and one of the few remaining wooden houses in the city nestle in the Begijnhof's secluded, tree-filled courtyard.

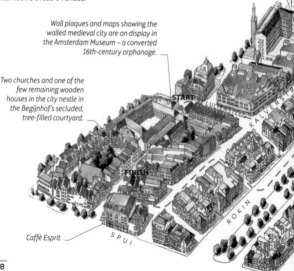

START

LUIJENSTEEG

KALVERSTR

FINISH

ROKIN

Caffè Esprit

SPUI

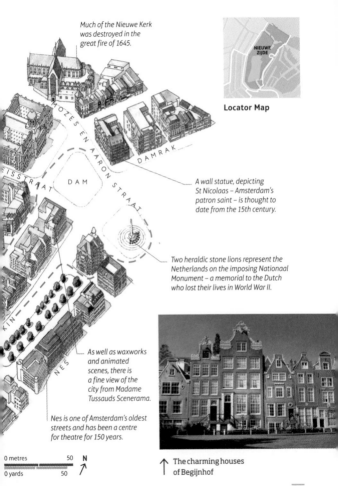

Much of the Nieuwe Kerk was destroyed in the great fire of 1645.

Locator Map

A wall statue, depicting St Nicolaas – Amsterdam's patron saint – is thought to date from the 15th century.

Two heraldic stone lions represent the Netherlands on the imposing Nationaal Monument – a memorial to the Dutch who lost their lives in World War II.

As well as waxworks and animated scenes, there is a fine view of the city from Madame Tussauds Scenerama.

Nes is one of Amsterdam's oldest streets and has been a centre for theatre for 150 years.

NIEUWE ZIJDE

MOZES EN AARON STRAAT

DAMRAK

DAM

EISSTRAAT

KIN

NES

0 metres 50
0 yards 50

N

↑ The charming houses of Begijnhof

OUDE ZIJDE

The "Old Side" is an oddball: an intensely urban quarter where piety and porn sit side by side. While the glow of the Red Light District almost bathes the 14th-century Oude Kerk, the smell of incense does battle with the all-too familiar scent of marijuana wafting down the streets.

The historic building lining the Oudezijds ↓ Voorburgwal canal

→

A visitor admiring an exhibition of Rembrandt's works, and the exterior of Rembrandt's home *(inset)*

Did You Know?

Rembrandt painted himself into many of his works as a spectator.

MUSEUM HET REMBRANDTHUIS

📍 G5 🏛 Jodenbreestraat 4 🚋 14 Ⓜ Nieuwmarkt 🕙 10am–6pm daily
📅 27 Apr, 25 Dec 🌐 rembrandthuis.nl

The former home of Amsterdam's most famous artist – creator of *The Nightwatch*, *The Anatomy Lesson of Dr Nicolaes Tulp* and over 300 other works – has been transformed into a sensitive museum allowing an intimate glimpse into the life and times of Rembrandt Harmenszoon van Rijn.

Rembrandt was an established portraitist, married to the daughter of a wealthy bourgeois family, when he bought this red-shuttered house on the edge of the Jewish district in 1639. By 1656, however, his fortunes had changed. No longer an artistic star, he was forced to sell his home.

Furnished according to the 1656 inventory, the house is now a museum dedicated to the artist. On the first floor is the studio where Rembrandt created many of his most famous works. A room on the mezzanine floor has some of his superb etchings on display, and the exhibition wing next door shows work by his contemporaries. Younger visitors will love the cabinet of curiosities on the second floor, with its stuffed crocodiles, narwhal tusks, skulls and fossils. Daily 17th-century etching and paint-mixing demonstrations – at no extra cost – enhance the experience.

OUDE KERK

📍 G4 🏠 Oudekerksplein 🚊 4, 24
🕐 10am-6pm Mon-Sat, 1-5:30pm Sun
🗓 27 Apr, 25 Dec 🌐 oudekerk.nl

Sitting incongruously in the heart of the Red Light District, the "Old Church" is Amsterdam's oldest and most stately monument.

The Oude Kerk dates from the mid-13th century, when a wooden church was built in a burial ground on a sand bank. The present Gothic structure is 14th century and has grown from a single-aisled church into a basilica. As it expanded, it became a gathering place for traders and a refuge for the poor. Its paintings and statuary were destroyed after the Alteration in 1578, but the rare gilded ceiling and stained-glass windows were undamaged. The world-famous organ was added in 1724. The church still holds services, but also hosts art exhibitions, performances and debates. The Oude Kerk is dedicated to St Nicholas, patron saint of the city.

2,500

tombstones are found in the church floor.

The spire of the bell tower was built in 1565, but the 47-bell carillon was added in 1658.

Great Organ

Tomb of Admiral Abraham van der Hulst, hero of the Second Anglo-Dutch War

Main entrance to church on Oudekerksplein

↑ The medieval Oude Kerk, a striking sight against the frenetic Red Light District

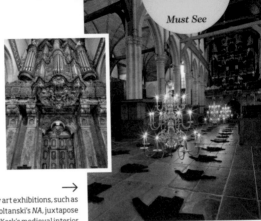

→ Christian Vater's oak-encased Great Organ, with its 4,000 pipes, is installed in the nave

→ Contemporary art exhibitions, such as Christian Boltanski's *NA*, juxtapose with the Oude Kerk's medieval interior

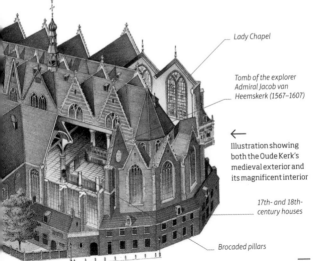

Lady Chapel

Tomb of the explorer Admiral Jacob van Heemskerk (1567–1607)

← Illustration showing both the Oude Kerk's medieval exterior and its magnificent interior

17th- and 18th-century houses

Brocaded pillars

JOODS HISTORISCH MUSEUM

📍H6 🏛Nieuwe Amstelstraat 1 🚋14 🎭Nationale Opera & Ballet Ⓜ Waterlooplein 🕐11am–5pm daily 🚫27 Apr, Yom Kippur and Jewish New Year 🌐jck.nl/en

From the first Jews to arrive in Amsterdam to the preservation of Jewish identity today, this museum tells the turbulent history of the Jewish community in the Netherlands.

The Collection

This remarkable museum of Jewish heritage is housed in four monumental synagogues – the Grote Synagoge, Nieuwe Synagoge, Obbene Shul and Dritt Shul. Three permanent multimedia exhibitions present the history and culture of the Jewish people in the Netherlands through paintings, drawings, artifacts, photographs, films and 3D displays. In addition, there are temporary exhibitions and a Children's Museum. This museum, the Portuguese Synagogue and the Hollandsche Schouwburg, form the Jewish Cultural Quarter.

The Nieuwe Synagoge (1752)

↑ The main entrance to the museum is through the stately Grote Synagoge

JEWS IN AMSTERDAM

The first Jew to gain Dutch citizenship was a member of the Portuguese Sephardic community in 1597. The Ashkenazi Jews from eastern Europe came to Amsterdam later, in the 1630s. They were restricted to working in certain trades, but were granted full civil equality in 1796. With the rise of Zionism in the 19th century, Jewish identity re-emerged, but the Nazi occupation almost obliterated the community.

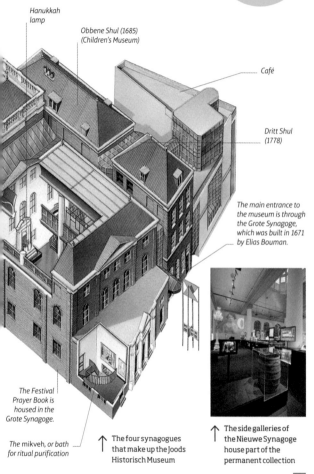

Hanukkah lamp

Obbene Shul (1685)
(Children's Museum)

Café

Dritt Shul
(1778)

The main entrance to
the museum is through
the Grote Synagoge,
which was built in 1671
by Elias Bouman.

The Festival
Prayer Book is
housed in the
Grote Synagoge.

The mikveh, or bath
for ritual purification

↑ The four synagogues
that make up the Joods
Historisch Museum

↑ The side galleries of
the Nieuwe Synagoge
house part of the
permanent collection

The imposing 15th-century Waag lit up at dusk

of the building. The ground floor is home to the café-restaurant In de Waag. Upstairs is the Waag Society, a research collective focusing on science, technology and the arts.

Agnietenkapel

◆ F5 **⌂** Oudezijds Voorburgwal 231 **🚊** 4, 14, 24 **⊘** To the public

The Agnietenkapel, which dates from 1470, was part of the convent of St Agnes until 1578, when it was closed after the Alteration. It is one of the few Gothic chapels to have survived this period of turmoil. In 1632, the Athenaeum Illustre, the precursor of the University of Amsterdam, took it over and by the mid-17th century it was a centre of scientific learning. It also housed the municipal library until the 1830s. During restoration from 1919 to 1921, elements of Amsterdam School architecture were introduced to the building. Despite these changes and long periods of secular use, the building still has the feel of a Franciscan chapel.

The large auditorium on the first floor is the

EXPERIENCE MORE

Waag

◆ G4 **⌂** Nieuwmarkt 4 **Ⓜ** Nieuwmarkt **ⓦ** waag.org

The multi-turreted Waag is Amsterdam's oldest surviving gatehouse. Built in 1488, it was then called St Antoniespoort. Public executions were held here, and prisoners awaited their fate in the "little gallows room". In 1617, the building became the public weigh house (*waaggebouw*); peasants had their produce weighed here and paid tax accordingly. Various guilds moved into the upper rooms of each tower, including the Guild of Surgeons, who from 1619 had their meeting room and anatomy theatre here. They added the central octagonal tower in 1691. Rembrandt's *Anatomy Lesson of Dr Nicolaes Tulp*, now in the Mauritshuis, and *The Anatomy Lesson of Dr Jan Deijman*, in the Amsterdam Museum, were commissioned by the guild.

After the weigh house closed in the early 1800s, the Waag served as a fire station and two city museums. But even into the first half of the 19th century, punishments were carried out in front city's oldest, and is used for university lectures. It has a lovely ceiling, painted with Renaissance motifs and a portrait of Minerva. A series of portraits of scholars – a gift from local merchant Gerardus van Papenbroeck in 1743 – also adorns the walls.

From 1921 until 2007, the chapel was home to the University Museum. It is now used as a conference centre and is not open to the public.

Nieuwmarkt

G4 **M** Nieuwmarkt
Antiques market: May–Sep: 9am–5pm Sun; Organic market: 9am–4pm Sat

An open, paved square, the Nieuwmarkt is flanked to the west by the Red Light District. Along with the top end of the Geldersekade, it forms Amsterdam's Chinatown. The Waag dominates the square, and construction of this gateway led to the site's development in the 15th century as a marketplace.

When the city expanded in the 17th century, the square took on its present

---

> Clothing stalls at the Nieuwmarkt, with the Waag in the background

---

RED LIGHT DISTRICT

Barely clad prostitutes bathed in a red neon glow and touting for business at their windows is one of the defining images of Amsterdam. The city's Red Light District, referred to locally as de Walletjes (the little walls), is concentrated around the Oude Kerk, although it extends as far as Warmoesstraat to the west, the Zeedijk to the north, the Kloveniersburgwal to the east and then along the line of Damstraat to the south.

Prostitution in Amsterdam dates back to the city's emergence as a port in the 13th century. By 1478, prostitution had become so widespread, with increasing numbers of sea-weary sailors flooding into the city, that attempts were made to contain it.

Today, hordes of visitors generate a buzz, and despite the sleaze, the council is making this area more culturally attractive, promoting the bars, eateries and beautiful canalside houses that punctuate the streets.

---

dimensions and was named the Nieuwmarkt. It retains an array of 17th- and 18th-century gabled houses and, true to tradition, antiques and organic markets are still held here.

The old Jewish Quarter leads off the square down St Antoniesbreestraat. In the 1970s, many houses in this area were demolished to make way for the metro, sparking clashes between protesters and police. The action of conservationists persuaded the city council to renovate rather than redevelop old buildings. In tribute to them, photographs of their protests decorate the metro.

Montelbaanstoren

🔲 H5 **🏠 Oudeschans 2**
Ⓜ Nieuwmarkt
🚪 To the public

The lower portion of the Montelbaanstoren was built in 1512 and formed part of Amsterdam's medieval fortifications. It lay just beyond the city wall, protecting the city's wharves on the newly built St Antoniesdijk (now the Oudeschans) from the neighbouring Gelderlanders.

The octagonal structure and open-work timber steeple were both added by Hendrick de Keyser in 1606. His decorative addition bears a close resemblance to the spire of the Oude Kerk, designed by Joost Bilhamer, which was built 40 years earlier. In 1611, the tower began to list, prompting Amsterdammers to attach ropes to the top and pull it right again.

Sailors from the VOC would gather at the Montelbaanstoren before being ferried in small boats down the IJ to the massive East Indies-bound sailing ships, anchored further out in deep water to the north.

The building, now housing Amsterdam's water authority, appears in a number of etchings by Rembrandt, and is still a popular subject for artists.

Zuiderkerk

🔲 G5 **🏠 Zuiderkerkhof 72** **🚇 14** **Ⓜ Nieuwmarkt**
🔲 Concerts only, check website; tower: closed for renovations, check website **🌐 zuiderkerk amsterdam.nl**

The Renaissance-style Zuiderkerk, designed by Hendrick de Keyser in 1603, was the first Calvinist church in Amsterdam after the Alteration. The spire, with its columns, decorative clocks and onion dome, is a prominent city landmark.

The Zuiderkerk ceased to function as a church in 1929 and it is now a meeting and congress centre. You can attend one of the venue's concerts, but the main reason to visit the Zuiderkerk is to climb the tower, which overlooks olive-green canals.

Stadhuis-Nationale Opera & Ballet

🔲 G6 **🏠 Waterlooplein 22**
📞 Stadhuis: 625 5455
🚇 14 **Ⓜ Waterlooplein**
🔲 Offices: 8:30am-8pm Mon-Fri **🌐 operaballet.nl**

Few buildings in Amsterdam caused as much controversy as the Stadhuis (town hall) and Nationale Opera & Ballet (opera house). Nicknamed the "Stopera" by protesters, the scheme required the destruction of dozens of medieval houses, which

---

DRINK

Café de Druif

Fragrant with four centuries of tobacco smoke and rum, Café de Druif may be the city's oldest tavern.

🔲 J5
🏠 Rapenburgerplein 83 **📞 624 4530**

Café de Engelbewaarder

Drop in to this traditional tavern on a Sunday for live jazz. Its arty habitués are lubricated by 15 brands of tasty beer from its taps.

🔲 G5
🏠 Kloveniersburgwal 59 **🌐 cafe-de-engelbewaarder.nl**

---

were virtually all that remained of the original Jewish quarter. This led to running battles between squatters and police.

Completed in 1986, the Nationale Opera & Ballet has the largest auditorium in the country, seating 1,689 people, and is home to the Netherlands' national opera and ballet companies. Book a ticket for a performance, take a backstage tour or, better yet, attend one of the free concerts at 12:30pm on Tuesdays from September to May.

NEMO Science Museum

📍 J4 📌 Oosterdok 2 🚌 22, 48 🚊 2, 4, 11, 12, 13, 14, 17, 24 Ⓜ Centraal Station 🕙 10am–5:30pm Tue-Sun (daily during school hols & Feb-Aug) 📅 27 Apr 🌐 nemo sciencemuseum.nl

In June 1997 the Netherlands' national science museum moved to this dazzling curved building, desiged by Renzo Piano, which protrudes 30 m (98 ft) over water. NEMO is the largest science museum in the Netherlands, with five floors filled with interactive exhibits, presenting technological innovations in a manner that allows both adults' and children's creativity full expression.

You can interact with virtual reality, operate the latest industrial equipment under expert supervision and harness science to produce your own art. Visitors – who in this setting might equally be termed explorers – can participate in experiments, demonstrations, games and workshops, or take in lectures, films and even educational stage shows.

The five floors are crammed full of fascinating exhibitions and fun activities. Discover new ways to enjoy mathematics in the World of Shapes; go on a voyage into space to learn more about the stars and the planets in Life in the Universe; or awaken a fascination for physics in Sensational Science.

NEMO Science Museum has the largest roof terrace in Amsterdam, with great views of the city. Piano designed the roof to resemble an Italian piazza and it provides the perfect spot to relax. Here you will also find an open-air exhibition and a restaurant. Access the roof via the lift from the central hall, or the stairs from street level, for free.

Check the website for special events, including live music and film screenings, held on the roof in spring and summer.

↓ The futuristic copper hull of NEMO Science Museum

Waterlooplein

📍H6 🚊14
Ⓜ Waterlooplein
🕐 Market: 9am–5pm
Mon–Fri, 8:30am–
5pm Sat

The Waterlooplein dates
from 1882, when two
canals were filled in to
create a large market
square. The site was originally called Vlooyenburg,
an artificial island built
in the 17th century to
house the Jewish settlers.

The original market
disappeared during
World War II when most
of the Jewish residents
of Amsterdam were trans-
ported by the Nazis to
concentration camps.
After the war, a popular
flea market grew up in
its place. Despite encroach-
ment by the Stadhuis-
Nationale Opera & Ballet,

the northern end of the
Waterlooplein still operates
a lively and interesting
market, selling anything
from bric-a-brac and
army-surplus clothing
to Balinese carvings.

Mozes en Aäronkerk

📍H6 Ⓐ Waterlooplein
205 🚊14 Ⓜ Waterlooplein
🕐 Prayer services: 8pm
Tue & Fri; Holy Mass: 5pm
Sun 🌐 santegidio.nl

Designed by the
Flemish architect T Suys
the Elder in 1841, Mozes
en Aäronkerk was built
on the site of a hidden
Catholic church. The
later church, with its two
towers, took its name
from the Old Testament
figures of Moses and
Aaron depicted on the
gable stones of the orig-

inal building. These are
now set into the rear wall.

The church was
restored in 1990, when
its twin wooden towers
were painted to look like
sandstone. After years
of hosting events, it is
again a place of worship.

Schreierstoren

📍H3 Ⓐ Prins
Hendrikkade 94–95
Ⓜ Centraal Station
🕐 10am–11pm daily
🌐 weepingtower.nl

Dating from 1480, the
Schreierstoren (Weepers'
Tower) was a defensive
structure forming part
of the medieval city walls.
It was one of the few
fortifications not to be
demolished as the city
expanded beyond its
medieval boundaries
in the 17th century. The
building now houses

Did You Know?

Amsterdam's nickname –
"Mokum" – means "place
of refuge" in Yiddish.

←

Decorated stalls
awaiting opening time at
Waterlooplein's flea market

the VOC café. Popular legend states that the tower derived its name from the weeping (*schreien* in the original Dutch) of women who came here to wave their men off to sea. It is more likely, however, that the title comes from the tower's position on a sharp (*screye* or *scherpe*) 90-degree bend in the old town walls. A wall plaque, dated 1569, adds considerably to the confusion by depicting a weeping woman alongside the inscription *srayer hovck*, which means "sharp corner".

In 1609, Henry Hudson set sail from here in an attempt to discover a new and faster trading route to the East Indies. Instead, he unintentionally "discovered" the river in North America that bears his name. A bronze plaque, laid in 1927, commemorates his voyage.

Portuguese Synagogue

📍 H6 🏠 Mr Visserplein 3
🚋 14 Ⓜ Waterlooplein
🕐 Feb-Nov: 10am-5pm Sun-Thu (to 4pm Fri Sep, Oct, Mar & Apr, to 2pm Fri Nov & Feb); Dec & Jan: 10am-4pm Sun-Thu (to 2pm Fri) 🚫 Jewish hols
🌐 jck.nl/en

The design for this synagogue, by Elias Bouman (1636–86), was inspired by the architecture of the Temple of Solomon in Jerusalem. Built for the Portuguese Sephardic community of Amsterdam and inaugurated in 1675, the huge building has a rectangular ground plan with the Holy Ark in the southeast corner facing Jerusalem, and the *tebah* (the podium from which the service is led) at the opposite end.

EAT

Greetje

Come here for elegant Dutch cuisine - stewed rabbit with sweet potato purée and *trekdrop* (liquorice) crème brûlée.

📍 J5 🏠 Peperstraat 23
🕐 L daily
🌐 restaurantgreetje.nl

In de Waag

This candlelit room in a 15th-century gatehouse is beautiful. The menu lists classic dishes.

📍 G4 🏠 Nieuwmarkt 4
🌐 indewaag.nl

Blauw aan de Wal

The eclectic menu features razor clams, oysters, buffalo ricotta and North Sea fish.

📍 G5 🏠 Oudezijds Achterburgwal 99
🕐 Mon & Sun
🌐 blauwaandewal.com

Café de Jaren

The restaurant's biggest selling point is its terrace overlooking the Amstel.

📍 F6 🏠 Nieuwe Doelenstraat 20
🌐 cafedejaren.nl

€€€

The wooden, barrel-vaulted ceiling is supported by four Ionic columns. The interior of the synagogue is illuminated by more than 1,000 candles. Treasure chambers in the basement contain a sumptuous collection of ceremonial objects made of silver, gold and silk brocades, and rare manuscripts. The synagogue is part of the city's Jewish Cultural Quarter.

A SHORT WALK

UNIVERSITY DISTRICT

Distance 1.5 km (1 mile) **Nearest metro** Nieuwmarkt **Time** 15 minutes

The University of Amsterdam, founded in 1877, is predominantly located in the peaceful, southwestern part of the Oude Zijde. A walk around the university district from Nieuwmarkt to the Agnietenkapel – where the university has its roots – takes in everything from the bustling Red Light District, where Damstraat meets the Nieuwmarkt, to the 15th-century Waag, which evokes a medieval air. As you head south of the Nieuwmarkt, stop off at Museum Het Rembrandt-huis for a fascinating insight into the life of the city's most famous artist.

Marijuana through the ages is explored at the Hash Marihuana & Hemp Museum.

START

FINISH

VOORBURGWAL

ACHTERBURGWAL

OUDE ZIJDS

This house, which was built in 1610, unusually faces three canals.

↑ The exterior of the Hash Marihuana & Hemp Museum

Originally part of a convent, the Agnietenkapel survived destruction during the Alteration, and got a new lease of life serving as the University of Amsterdam's first lecture hall.

The large Oudemanhuispoort was built in the 18th century to function as an almshouse for elderly men.

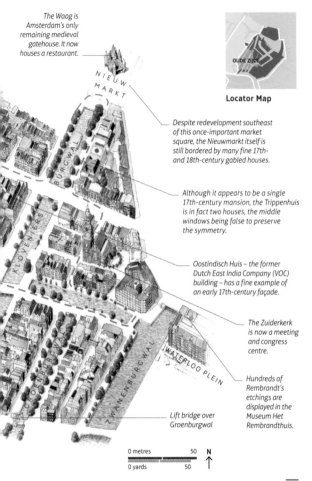

The Waag is Amsterdam's only remaining medieval gatehouse. It now houses a restaurant.

Locator Map

Despite redevelopment southeast of this once-important market square, the Nieuwmarkt itself is still bordered by many fine 17th- and 18th-century gabled houses.

Although it appears to be a single 17th-century mansion, the Trippenhuis is in fact two houses, the middle windows being false to preserve the symmetry.

Oostindisch Huis – the former Dutch East India Company (VOC) building – has a fine example of an early 17th-century façade.

The Zuiderkerk is now a meeting and congress centre.

Hundreds of Rembrandt's etchings are displayed in the Museum Het Rembrandthuis.

Lift bridge over Groenburgwal

| 0 metres | 50 |
| 0 yards | 50 |

N
↑

CENTRAL CANAL RING

Curving between the IJ and the Amstel like concentric ripples in a pond, the Singel, Herengracht, Keizersgracht and Prinsengracht canals define Amsterdam's central canal ring. Compared with the cramped Nieuwe Zijde, there's a more spacious feel to this part of the city. Leidseplein – the area's hub – is packed with open-air cafés, but the square really comes into its own after dark, when music bars and dance clubs attract throngs of visitors and a sprinkling of locals. In summer, the party scene spills out onto the waterside streets, giving the area a fizzing atmosphere.

Art Deco interior of
Café Americain ↓

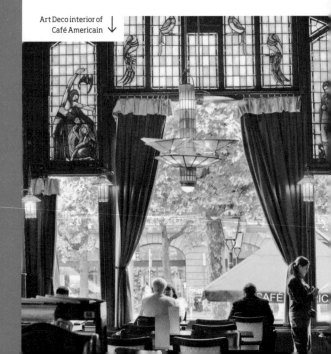

ANNE FRANK HOUSE

D4 🏠 Westermarkt 58 🚊 13, 17 🕐 Apr-Oct: 9am-10pm daily; Nov-Mar: 9am-7pm daily (to 9pm Sat) 🚫 Yom Kippur 🌐 annefrank.org

Anne Frank's diary is a moving portrait of a little girl growing up in times of oppression. Even those who have not read her diary will be moved by the annexe where she and her family hid.

↑ Photos of Anne - happy and carefree - before she went into hiding

On 6 July 1942, to avoid their Nazi persecutors, the Jewish Frank family moved from Merwedeplein to the rear annexe of the warehouse at Prinsengracht 263. Anne, her mother Edith, her father Otto and her older sister Margot lived here, along with the Van Pels family and dentist Fritz Pfeffer. It was here that Anne wrote her famous diary. On 4 August 1944, the annexe was raided by the Gestapo. All those hiding were arrested and taken to different Nazi concentration camps. The building beside Anne Frank House holds exhibitions exploring all forms of persecution and discrimination, as well as explaining Anne's story. It is the almost empty annexe, however, which conveys the realities of persecution. Tickets are only available online; it is advisable to book well in advance.

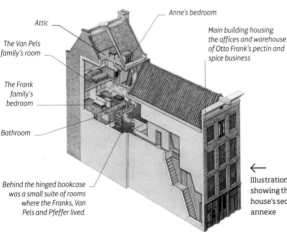

Attic

The Van Pels family's room

The Frank family's bedroom

Bathroom

Behind the hinged bookcase was a small suite of rooms where the Franks, Van Pels and Pfeffer lived.

Anne's bedroom

Main building housing the offices and warehouse of Otto Frank's pectin and spice business

← Illustration showing the house's secret annexe

EXPERIENCE MORE

Stadsschouwburg

📍 D7 🏠 Leidseplein 26
🚊 1, 2, 5, 7, 11, 12, 19
🕐 Box office: noon–6pm
Mon–Sat; two hours
before performance Sun
🌐 ssba.nl

This Neo-Renaissance
building, dating from
1894, is the most recent
of three successive muni-
cipal theatres in the city,
its predecessors having
burned down. The theatre
was designed by Jan
Springer (1850–1915),
whose other credits include
the Frascati building on
Oxford Street in London,
and A L van Gendt (1835–
1901), who was also responsible for the Concertgebouw
and for part of Centraal
Station. The planned orna-
mentation of the theatre's
red-brick exterior was
never carried out because
of budget cuts. This, com-
bined with a hostile public
reaction to his theatre,
forced a disillusioned
Springer into virtual retire-
ment. Public disgust was
due, however, to the theatre
management's policy of
restricting use of the front
door to patrons who had
bought expensive tickets.
The whole building has
since been given a face-lift.

Until the Nationale
Opera & Ballet was com-
pleted in 1986, the

Stadsschouwburg was
home to the Dutch
national ballet and opera
companies. Today, the
theatre stages plays from
local artistic groups such
as the resident Toneelgroep
Amsterdam, and inter-
national companies,
including some English-
language productions.

An auditorium, located
between the Melkweg and
the Stadsschouwburg, is

SHOP

De Negen Straajes

The Singel bounds
this rectangle of nine
small shopping
streets to the east and
the Prinsengracht
borders it to the west.
The "Nine Streets"
are filled with
designer boutiques
and vintage stores.
Be sure to check
out Laura Dols
at Wolvenstraat 7,
which specializes
in the 1950s, and
I Love Vintage at
Prinsengracht 201.

📍 E5

25,000

bicycles end up in
Amsterdam's canals
every year.

used by both centres for
large-scale performances.

Het Grachtenhuis

📍 E6 🏠 Herengracht 386
🚊 2, 11, 12 🕐 10am–5pm
Tue–Sun (daily Jun–Aug)
🗓 27 Apr, 25 Dec
🌐 hetgrachtenhuis.nl

This ornate canal house was
designed in 1663 and 1665
by Philips Vingboons (1607–
78), the architect of the
Cromhouthuis – Bijbels
Museum. Once the former
home of merchants and
bankers, the house is now
the Museum of the Canals.
Using fun interactive displays, it tells the story of
town planning and engi-
neering for the creation of
Amsterdam's triple canal
ring. The ground floor has
been restored to its 18th-
century splendour, complete
with original wall paintings.
The museum's upper rooms
showcase detailed models,
films and 3D animation
on the construction of
the canals, along with the
stately mansions that line
the route.

De Krijtberg

📍 E6 🏠 Singel 448
🚋 2, 11, 12 🕐 Noon–
1:15pm & 5–6:15pm
Mon & Fri, noon–
6:15pm Tue–Thu &
Sat, 9am–6:30pm Sun
🌐 krijtberg.nl

An impressive Neo-Gothic church, the Krijtberg (chalk hill) replaced a clandestine Jesuit chapel in 1884. It is officially known as Franciscus Xaveriuskerk, after St Francis Xavier, one of the founding Jesuit priests. Designed by Alfred Tepe (1840–1920), the church was constructed on the site of three houses; the presbytery beside the church is on the site of two other houses, one of which had belonged to a chalk merchant – hence the church's nickname.

The back of the church is wider than the front. The narrowness of the façade is redeemed by its two magnificent, steepled towers, which soar to 17 m (55 ft). The ornate interior of the building has spectacular lighting and contains some good examples of Neo-Gothic design. The stained-glass windows, walls painted in bright colours and liberal use of gold are in striking contrast to the city's austere Protestant churches.

A statue of St Francis Xavier stands to the front left of the high altar; one of St Ignatius, founder of the Jesuits, stands to the right.

The colourful interior of De Krijtberg ↑

Cromhouthuis - Bijbels Museum

📍 E6 🏠 Herengracht 366-368 🚊 2, 11, 12 🚊 Herengracht/ Leidsegracht 🕐 10am-5pm daily 🗓 27 Apr 🌐 cromhouthuis.nl

This canal house, and the one next door, were owned by the Cromhout family, eminent Amsterdam citizens in the 17th and 18th centuries. They were avid art collectors, and the houses have been restored to recreate their eclectic collection of portraits and curiosities. Two of the salons have fine ceiling paintings by Jacob de Wit, and other features include two well-preserved 17th-century kitchens. The top floors house the Biblical Museum, which is packed with artifacts that aim to give historical weight to biblical stories. Displays have models of historical sites, and highlights include a copy of the Book of Isaiah from the Dead Sea Scrolls and the Delft Bible, dating from 1477. The museum has a lovely garden.

Felix Meritis Building

📍 D5 🏠 Keizersgracht 324 🚊 2, 11, 12, 13, 17 🕐 For renovation until late 2019 🌐 felixmeritis.nl

This Neo-Classical building is best viewed from the opposite side of the canal. Designed by Jacob Otten Husly, it opened in 1787 as a science and arts centre set up by the Felix Meritis society. The name means "happiness through merit". An association of wealthy citizens, the society was founded by the watchmaker Willem Writs in 1777, at the time of the Dutch Enlightenment. Five reliefs on the façade proclaim the society's interest in natural science and art. The building was fitted out with an observatory, library, laboratories and a small concert hall. Mozart, Grieg, Brahms and Saint-Saëns are among the many distinguished musicians who have given performances in the society's hall.

In the 19th century, it became Amsterdam's main cultural centre, and its concert hall inspired the design of the Concertgebouw.

The Dutch Communist Party (CPN) occupied the premises from 1946, but cultural prominence was restored in the 1970s when the Shaffy Theatre Company used the building as a theatre and won

 HIDDEN GEM
Homomonument

The pink triangle used to "brand" homosexual men during World War II influenced Karin Daan's 1987 design of this memorial to oppressed gay men and women. The seating provides a quiet place of contemplation amid the bustle of Westermarkt.

 The Palladian façade of the 18th-century Felix Meritis Building

acclaim for its avant-garde productions. In 1988 the building housed the European Centre for Arts and Sciences. It is undergoing extensive renovation and will reopen once more as a cultural centre in spring 2020.

Westerkerk

📍D4 🏠Prinsengracht 281 🚊13, 17 ⏰Church: Nov-Mar: 10am-3pm Mon-Fri; Apr-Oct: 10am-3pm Mon-Sat; tower tours: Apr-Oct: 10am-7:30pm Mon-Sat 🌐westerkerk.nl

This is the most beautiful of the four churches built to the north, south, east and west of the city's core in the 17th century as part of the development of the Canal Ring. It has the tallest tower in the city at 85 m (272 ft) high, and the largest nave of any Dutch Protestant church. It was designed by Hendrick de Keyser, who died in 1621, a year after work began.

Rembrandt was buried here, though his grave has never been found. The shutters of the huge organ (1686) were painted, by Gérard de Lairesse, with scenes showing King David,

↑ Westerkerk, standing proudly alongside the Keizersgracht canal

the Queen of Sheba and the Evangelists. The spire of the Westerkerk, which is built in tapering sections, is topped by the Imperial Crown of Maximilian.

The panoramic views of Amsterdam from the top of the tower justify the rather gruelling climb. The church is undergoing restoration and sections may be closed during this time.

Leidsegracht

D6 1, 2, 5, 7, 11, 12, 19

The Leidsegracht was for a few years the main route for barges from Amsterdam to Leiden. It was cut in 1664 to a plan by city architect Daniel Stalpaert, and stretches for only four blocks between the grand Herengracht and the long Singelgracht, the outermost of Amsterdam's canal rings. Despite its small size, it is now one of the city's most desirable addresses. Townhouses for sale here start at around €2 million. Cornelis Lely, who drew up the original plans for draining the Zuiderzee, was born at No 39 in 1854. A wall plaque shows Lely poised between the Zuiderzee and the newly created IJsselmeer.

Golden Bend

E6 2, 11, 12, 24

Kattenkabinet: 10am–5pm Mon–Fri, noon–5pm Sat & Sun 1 Jan, 27 Apr, 25 Dec

The stretch of the Herengracht between Leidsestraat and Vijzelstraat was first called the Golden Bend in the 17th century, because of the great wealth of the shipbuilders, merchants and politicians who originally lived along here. Most of the mansions have been converted into offices, but their former elegance

> **Did You Know?**
>
> Canal houses tilt to allow goods to be winched to the attic without crashing into the windows.

Grand mansions lining the Leidsegracht ↑

remains. The majority of the buildings are faced with sandstone, which was more expensive than brick.

The earliest mansions date from the 1660s. One very fine example of the Classicist style, designed by Philips Vingboons in 1664, stands at No 412. Building continued into the 18th century, with the Louis XIV style predominating; built in 1730, No 475 is typical of this trend and it is often called the jewel of canal houses. Two sculpted female figures over the front door adorn its sandstone façade. The

CANAL-HOUSE ARCHITECTURE

Amsterdam has been called a city of "well-mannered" architecture because its charms lie in intimate details rather than in grand effects. From the 15th century on, planning laws, plot sizes and the instability of the topsoil dictated that façades were largely uniform in size and built of lightweight brick or sandstone, with large windows to reduce the weight. As a result of this, owners stamped their own individuality on the buildings through the use of decorative gables, ornate doorcases and varying window shapes. Carved and painted wall plaques were used to identify houses before street numbering was introduced.

ornate mansion at No 452 is a good example of a 19th-century conversion. The Kattenkabinet (Cat Museum) at No 497 Herengracht is one of the few houses on the Golden Bend that is accessible to the public and is a must-visit for fans of all things feline.

A SHORT WALK
LEIDSEBUURT

*Archaeological finds from
Egypt are on display at
the Cromhouthuis –
Bijbels Museum.*

Distance 2 km (1.5 miles) **Nearest tram** 2, 11,
12 (Koningsplein) **Time** 20 minutes

The area around Leidseplein is one of Amsterdam's
busiest nightspots. There are plays to be seen at the
Stadsschouwburg and music to be heard at Melkweg.
But this area also has plenty to offer on a daytime walk.
There is fine architecture to admire around the Canal
Ring, such as the Former City Orphanage on Prinsengracht,
the lavish De Krijtberg on the Singel and scores of
grand houses on the Golden Bend.

*Het Grachtenhuis is a museum that tells
the story of Amsterdam's canal ring.*

*Cut in 1664, the Leidsegracht
was the main waterway for
barges heading for Leiden.*

*This once housed Amsterdam's
orphans and the Court of Appeal.*

*Young people flock to Leidseplein
to watch street performances
and enjoy the vibrant nightlife.*

*This converted milk-processing
factory survives as Melkweg, one
of Amsterdam's key venues for
alternative entertainment.*

*A historic theatre, Stadsschouwburg
is one of the venues for Amsterdam's
Holland Festival in June.*

*The American Hotel's Café
Americain has a fine Art Deco
interior and is a popular place
to while away an afternoon.*

FINISH

START

De Krijtberg – an impressive Neo-Gothic church – houses an ornate wooden carving of the Immaculate Conception.

Locator Map

Classical columns and façades on the Herengracht's Golden Bend powerfully recall the city's wealth.

0 metres 50
0 yards 50

N

↑ Buzzy open-air cafés on Leidseplein

MUSEUM QUARTER

For lovers of high culture, the Museumplein is what Amsterdam is all about. Three world-class museums and one of the world's great concert halls stand around a calm green space. Visitors flock here to the square to pose for photographs, admire Old Masters in the Rijksmuseum and modernists in the Stedelijk Museum, but the Van Gogh Museum is the quarter's true star. Away from the Museumplein, you'll find elegant streets defined by wealth and taste.

The ever-expanding Rijksmuseum's ↓ bike tunnel

Visitors milling around
the entrance hall of the
Van Gogh Museum

VAN GOGH MUSEUM

◉ D9 **⌂ Museumplein 6** **🚋 2, 3, 5, 12** **◷ Jan, Feb, Nov & Dec: 9am-9pm Fri, 9am-5pm Sat-Thu; Mar-Jun, Sep & Oct: 9am-9pm Fri, 9am-6pm Sat-Thu; Jul & Aug: 9am-9pm Fri & Sat, 9am-7pm Sun-Thu**
ⓦ vangoghmuseum.com

When Van Gogh died in 1890, he was on the verge of stardom. His brother Theo, an art dealer, amassed a collection of 200 of his paintings and 500 drawings. These, with around 850 letters by the artist, form the core of the world's largest Van Gogh collection.

The Van Gogh Museum is based on a design by De Stijl architect Gerrit Rietveld (1888–1964) and opened in 1973. A freestanding wing, designed by Kisho Kurokawa, was added in 1999.

The ground floor shows Van Gogh's self-portraits chronologically. Paintings from his Dutch and French periods are on the first floor, along with works by other 19th-century artists. The second floor focuses on Van Gogh's personal life, with a selection of letters. Works from his last year are shown on the third floor, as well as works by later artists who were influenced by him. The main entrance is through the Exhibition Wing, which houses temporary exhibitions. Every Friday night the central hall is turned into a bar with lounge chairs and DJs.

AN ARTIST'S LIFE

Vincent van Gogh (1853–90), born in Zundert, began painting in 1880. He worked in the Netherlands for five years before moving to Paris, later settling in the south of France. After an argument with Gauguin, he cut off part of his own ear and his mental instability forced him into an asylum in Saint-Rémy. He sought help in Auvers, where he shot himself, dying two days later.

RIJKSMUSEUM

📍 D8 🏠 Museumstraat 1 🚊 1, 2, 5, 7, 12, 19 🚋 Stadhouderskade
🕐 9am–5pm daily (garden, shop and café to 6pm) 🌐 rijksmuseum.nl

The Rijksmuseum is a familiar Amsterdam landmark and possesses an unrivalled collection of Dutch art, begun in the early 19th century. The vast museum can seem overwhelming, but with such a wealth of things to see, it's no wonder that it's the city's most-visited museum.

The Rijksmuseum began life as the Nationale Kunstgalerij in Den Haag. In 1808, King Louis Napoleon ordered the collection to be moved to Amsterdam and it briefly occupied the Koninklijk Paleis before it moved to its present location in 1885.

The red-brick building, designed by P J H Cuypers, was initially criticized, most vehemently by Amsterdam's Protestant community for its Catholic Neo-Renaissance style. King William III famously refused to set foot inside.

Nowadays, the building is fondly regarded and it forms the background of many of the images taken by novice photographers in the city due to its iconic exterior and beautifully tended gardens, which make for the perfect shot in every season.

> 💬 INSIDER TIP
> **Beat the Queue**
>
> The only way to walk straight inside the museum is to book a guided tour. Otherwise, get there at 9am or 3:30pm, and avoid Fridays and weekends.

↑ The Gallery of Honour is lined with Golden Age masterpieces

← The red-brick, Neo-Renaissance façade of the Rijksmuseum

TOP 5 UNMISSABLE EXHIBITS

The Night Watch (1642)
This vast canvas was commissioned by an Amsterdam militia.

The Kitchen Maid (1658)
The stillness and light are typical of Vermeer.

St Elizabeth's Day Flood (1500)
An unknown artist painted a flood in 1421.

The Square Man (1951)
This painting is typical of Appel's CoBrA work.

Shiva Nataraja (c 1100–1200)
This bronze statue shows the god dancing.

STEDELIJK MUSEUM

📍 C9 🏛 Museumplein 10 🚊 2, 3, 5, 12 🕙 10am-6pm daily (to 10pm Fri) 🌐 stedelijk.nl

Built to house a collection left to the city by Sophia de Bruyn in 1890, the Stedelijk Museum became the national museum of modern art and design in 1938, displaying works by artists such as Picasso, Matisse, Mondriaan, Chagall and Cézanne, and designers including Rietveld, Wirkkala and Sottsass.

The museum is housed in two contrasting spaces. The Neo-Renaissance main building was designed by A W Weissman (1858–1923) in 1895. The façade is adorned with turrets and gables and with niches containing statues of artists and architects, including Hendrick de Keyser and Jacob van Campen, architect of the Koninklijk Paleis. The Stedelijk's modern addition – the Benthem Crouwel Wing – opened in 2012. The giant "bathtub" appears to float, given its continuous glass walls at ground level; it remains a love-it-or-loathe-it addition to the city's

↑ The futuristic Benthem Crouwel Wing - or the "bathtub" - illuminated in the evening

architecture. Inside, both spaces are ultramodern, providing the perfect backdrop for the museum's 90,000 modern and contemporary artworks. The collection represents virtually every artistic movement of the 20th and 21st centuries, including examples of the De Stijl, Pop Art and CoBrA groups. It also houses a small group of works by Post-Impressionists, including Van Gogh and Cézanne, to highlight the late 19th century. The museum holds collections from present-day artists in a larger exhibition space, with a restaurant and a terrace overlooking Museumplein. The museum also stages performances and film screenings.

←

The Fiddler (1912-13), by Marc Chagall (1887-1985), was inspired by the artist's memories of St Petersburg and his new surroundings in Paris

1988
—
Three paintings by Van Gogh, Jongkind and Cézanne were stolen from the museum.

↑ The light and airy space that houses the museum's shop

EXPERIENCE MORE

Moco Museum

📍 D8 🏛 Honthorststraat 20 🚊 1, 2, 5, 7, 12, 19 🚋 Stadhouderskade ⏰ 10am–6pm daily; check website for later openings 🌐 mocomuseum.com

The exterior of this beautiful 20th-century mansion, designed by Eduard Cuypers, the nephew of P J H Cuypers, belies the groundbreaking collection housed inside.

Carefully curated by private collectors, the groundbreaking Modern Contemporary (Moco) Museum displays pieces by artists who expose the irony at work in modern society. The museum aims to show visitors what cannot be seen anywhere else.

The collection includes Roy Lichtenstein's pop art and more than 90 original works by the street artist Banksy. The British activist's indoor pieces are far less exposed than his usual murals and make for an interesting contrast when compared to the few works rescued from buildings that are also on display here.

→

Concertgebouw façade sparkling after dark

Concertgebouw

📍 C9 🏛 Concertgebouwplein 10 🚊 2, 3, 5, 12 🎫 Box office: 1–7pm Mon–Fri, 10am–7pm Sat & Sun 🌐 concertgebouw.nl

Following an open architectural competition held in 1881, A L van Gendt (1835–1901) was chosen to design a vast new concert hall for Amsterdam. The resulting Neo-Renaissance building boasts an elaborate pediment and colonnaded façade, and houses two concert halls. Despite Van Gendt's lack of musical knowledge, he managed to produce near-perfect acoustics in the Grote Zaal (main concert hall), which is renowned the world over. The inaugural concert at the Concertgebouw was held on 11 April 1888, complete with an orchestra of 120 musicians and a choir of 600. Though primarily designed to hold concerts, the building has become multifunctional; it has played host to exhibitions, political meetings and occasional boxing matches. Take a guided tour at 5pm on Friday or 12:30pm on Sunday to hear about the secret history of the building. For the best experience, visit on a Wednesday and take the 1:30pm tour after enjoying a free concert (not available in July and August).

VondelCS

📍 C8 🏛 Vondelpark 3 🚊 1, 3, 5, 11, 12 🌐 vondelpark3.nl

Vondelpark's pavilion opened in 1881 as a

INSIDER TIP
Rollerblading in Vondelpark

Don rollerblades for a different way of exploring Vondelpark's network of cycle paths. Rent wheels or book a training session with Skate Dokter (www.skatedokter.nl).

restaurant and café. A flamboyant, Neo-Renaissance-style building, it was the favourite haunt of Amsterdam's bohemian crowd, and its salons often featured contemporary art exhibitions. After World War II, the pavilion became a cultural centre and from 1972 it was the home of the Filmmuseum, which became the EYE.

The pavilion reopened in 2014 as VondelCS, and is now home to AVROTROS, one of the Netherlands' public broadcasting corporations. It hosts talk shows, concerts and debates on culture and current affairs. The ground floor of the pavilion is a café-restaurant called Vondelpark3.

↑ Cyclists taking a rest beside the lake in Vondelpark

Vondelpark

⊙ A9
🏛 Stadhouderskade
🚊 1, 2, 3, 5, 11, 12
⊙ Open-air theatre: Jun-last week Aug: Wed-Sun 🌐 openlucht theater.nl

In 1864, a group consisting of prominent Amsterdammers formed a committee with the aim of founding a public park, and they raised enough money to buy 8 ha (20 acres) of land. J D and L P Zocher, a father-and-son team of landscape architects, were then commissioned to design the park. They used vistas, pathways and ponds to create the illusion of a large natural area, which was opened on 15 June 1865 as the Nieuwe Park.

The park's present name was adopted in 1867, when a statue of Dutch poet Joost van den Vondel was erected here. The committee soon began to raise money to enlarge the park, and by June 1877 it had reached its current dimensions of 47 ha (116 acres). The park now supports around 100 plant species and 127 types of tree. Squirrels, hedgehogs, ducks and garden birds mix with a huge colony of greedy, bright-green parakeets, which gather in front of the pavilion every morning to be fed. Herds of cows, sheep, goats and even a lone llama graze in the pastures.

Vondelpark welcomes more than ten million visitors a year. Free concerts are given by *openluchttheater* (open-air theatre), and musicians play at the bandstand in the summer.

JOOST VAN DEN VONDEL

Joost van den Vondel (1587-1679) was to Dutch poetry and drama what Rembrandt was to painting. Many of his history plays, like *Gijsbrecht van Amstel*, first performed in 1638, and *Joannes de Boetgezant* (1662), were hailed as masterpieces. After converting to his wife's Catholic faith, he became an advocate of religious tolerance. That made him unpopular with hardline Calvinists and, despite his fame, he died an impoverished man.

Coster Diamonds

📍 D8 🏠 Paulus Potterstraat 2-6 🚊 2, 5, 12 🕐 9am-5pm daily 🌐 coster diamonds.com

Coster was founded in 1840. Twelve years later, Queen Victoria's consort, Prince Albert, gave the company the task of repolishing the enormous Koh-i-Noor (mountain of light) diamond. This blue-white stone is one of the treasures of the British crown

jewels and weighs in at 108.8 carats. A replica of the coronation crown, with a copy of the fabulous stone, is found in Coster's entrance hall.

More than 6,000 people visit the factory each week to witness the processes of grading, cutting and polishing the stones. Goldsmiths and diamond-cutters work together to produce customized items of jewellery, which are available over the counter. For serious diamond-buyers, such as the jewellers who come to Amsterdam from all over the world, there is a series of private sales rooms where discretion is assured. A few doors down is a small museum, in which the history of the diamond is traced.

AMSTERDAM'S MILITIA COMPANIES

The Dutch *schutterij* (militia companies) were formed in medieval times. Armed with bows, the forces' purpose was to protect towns from attack and revolts. By the 17th century, they carried muskets, but their role had become ceremonial. Captains had to be wealthy, as they equipped volunteers out of their own purse. They commissioned portraits and Rembrandt's *The Guard Company of Captain Frans Banning Cocq and Lieutenant Willem Ruytenburch* - known as *The Night Watch* - is the most famous. A statue of the painting is found in Rembrandtplein.

Hollandsche Manege

📍 B8 🏠 Vondelstraat 140 🚊 2 🕐 10am-5pm daily 🔒 2 weeks in Aug (see website for details) 🌐 levend paardenmuseum.nl

The Dutch Riding School was originally situated on the Leidsegracht, but in 1882 it moved to a new building on Vondelstraat. Designed by A L van Gendt, it was based on the Spanish Riding School in Vienna. The Hollandsche Manege was threatened with

demolition in the 1980s, but fortunately it was saved after a public outcry. Reopened in 1986 by Prince Bernhard, it has been restored to its former glory.

The Neo-Classical indoor arena boasts gilded mirrors and moulded horses' heads on its elaborate plasterwork walls. Some of the wrought-iron stalls remain and sound is muffled by sawdust. At the top of the staircase, one door leads to a balcony overlooking the arena, another to the café.

Vondelkerk

📍 B8 🏠 Vondelstraat 120 🚊 2

The Vondelkerk was the largest church designed by P J H Cuypers. Work began on the building in 1872, but funds ran out by the following year. Money from public donations and lotteries allowed it to be completed by 1880. When fire broke out in 1904, firefighters saved the nave of the church by forcing the burning tower to fall away into Vondelpark.

A new tower was added later by the architect's son, J T Cuypers. The church was deconsecrated in 1979 and converted into offices in 1985. It hosts concerts and events.

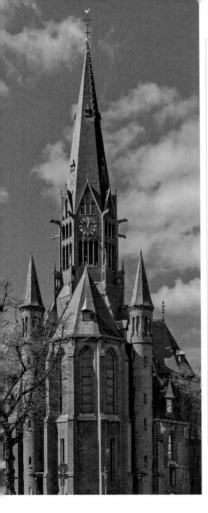

EAT

Cobra Café
Famous for its apple pie, Cobra also serves pancakes and other snacks, such as croquettes.

 D8
 Hobbemastraat 18
 cobracafe.nl

€€€

'T Blauwe Theehuis
This Vondelpark landmark serves drinks and toasted sandwiches.

 B8 Vondelpark 5
 blauwetheehuis.nl

€€€

Momo
This stylish bar-cum-restaurant offers sushi or set menus of ten dishes.

 D8 Hobbemastraat 1 momo-amsterdam.com

 €€€

←

The Vondelkerk, at the edge of Vondelpark

A SHORT WALK
MUSEUM QUARTER

Distance 1.5 km (1 mile) **Nearest tram** 2, 3, 5, 12 (Rijksmuseum) **Time** 15 minutes

The green expanse of Museumplein was once bisected by a busy road known locally as the "shortest motorway in Europe". Renovation transformed it into a park, fringed by Amsterdam's major cultural centres. Traverse one of the wealthiest districts in the city, with wide streets lined with grand houses. After the heady delights of the museums, why not window-shop at the boutiques along the PC Hooftstraat and Van Baerlestraat, or watch the diamond polishers at work in Coster Diamonds?

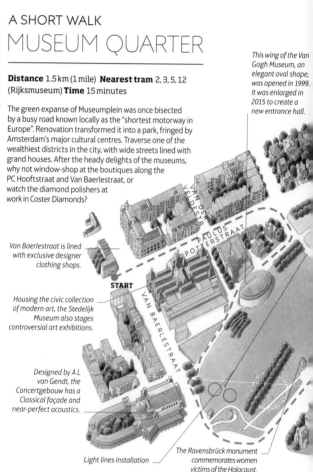

This wing of the Van Gogh Museum, an elegant oval shape, was opened in 1999. It was enlarged in 2015 to create a new entrance hall.

Van Baerlestraat is lined with exclusive designer clothing shops.

START

Housing the civic collection of modern art, the Stedelijk Museum also stages controversial art exhibitions.

Designed by A L van Gendt, the Concertgebouw has a Classical façade and near-perfect acoustics.

Light lines installation

The Ravensbrück monument commemorates women victims of the Holocaust.

Diamonds have been cut, polished and sold at Coster Diamonds since 1840. The firm now occupies three splendid adjoining villas, built on Museumplein in 1896.

Locator Map

FINISH

The heavily ornamented Neo-Renaissance Rijksmuseum holds the magnificent Dutch national art collection of paintings, applied art and historical artifacts.

The Rijksmuseum is surrounded by beautiful gardens filled with statuary. As well as 19th-century bronzes, you will find modern works made from surprising materials here.

Pond/ice rink

N ↑

→ The modern exterior of the Van Gogh Museum

EASTERN CANAL RING

The Singel and the Amstel canals define this district, while Vijzelstraat and Vijzelgracht cut a straight line through its heart. At the north end of Vijzelstraat is a sight much loved by visitors – the Bloemenmarkt, with its floating flower vendors. South of Singelgracht – in the De Pijp area – the landscape changes. Striking modern architecture replaces the graceful Golden Age canal-house façades. This is Amsterdam's most multicultural neighbourhood and Albert Cuypmarkt sits at its core, where the air is clouded with enticing scents and vendors call to passersby.

↓ Flowers hanging in the Bloemenmarkt

MUSEUM WILLET-HOLTHUYSEN

📍 G6 🏠 Herengracht 605 🚊 4, 14 🕐 10am–5pm daily
🚫 27 Apr 🌐 willetholthuysen.nl

A visit to Amsterdam wouldn't be complete without exploring one of the city's iconic canal houses. Named after its last residents, the Museum Willet-Holthuysen allows the visitor a glimpse into the lives of the emerging merchant class who lived in luxury along the Grachtengordel (Canal Ring) in the 17th century. Three floors, and the formal garden, are open to the public.

The house was built in 1685 for Jacob Hop, mayor of Amsterdam. It became the property of coal magnate Pieter Holthuysen (1788–1858) in 1855. It then passed to his daughter Louisa (1824–95) and her husband, Abraham Willet (1825–88), who were both fervent collectors of paintings, glass, silver and ceramics. When Louisa died childless and a widow in 1895, the house and its many treasures were left to the city on the condition that it became a museum bearing their names. Room by room, the house is being restored and brought back to the time Abraham and Louisa lived here.

Arguably, the most interesting part of the house is found below stairs. Special exhibits illuminating the lives of the Willet-Holthuysens' servants are displayed on the lower floor.

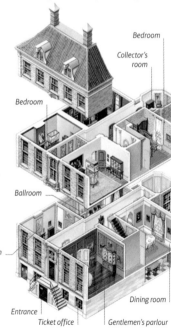

→

The Museum Willet-Holthuysen's rooms, ranging from a functional kitchen in the basement to a frivolous collector's room on the first floor

Bedroom

Collector's room

Bedroom

Ballroom

Front room

Entrance

Ticket office

Dining room

Gentlemen's parlour

EXPERIENCE MORE

Foam Museum

⦿ F7 🏠 **Keizersgracht 609** 🚊 **24** Ⓜ **Vijzelgracht** 🕐 **10am–6pm Sat–Wed, 10am–9pm Thu & Fri** 📅 **27 Apr** 🌐 **foam.org**

Three elegant 17th-century canal houses on the Keizersgracht have been joined together and beautifully renovated to create this labyrinth of modern rooms filled with photographs. Over 20,000 visitors flock here annually, making it the most-visited photography museum in the Netherlands by far.

Foam (Fotografiemuseum Amsterdam) is dedicated to exhibiting and celebrating every form of photography, from historical to journalistic, cutting-edge to artistic. The museum has an international outlook – photographs exhibited here are taken all over the world by photographers from a variety of cultures and ethnic backgrounds.

The museum holds four major exhibitions a year and 15 smaller ones, showcasing both established figures of the art form and emerging local talent. Exhibitions at Foam have included Annie Leibovitz's "American Music", a retrospective on Henri Cartier-Bresson and "50 Years of World Press Photo".

More than just a museum, though, Foam prides itself on being an interactive centre for photography, a place where amateurs can learn more about the art by meeting professionals, attending lectures and taking part in discussion evenings, or just stop for a coffee and a browse of the well-stocked bookshop. Foam also hosts pop-up exhibitions in different neighbourhoods to make photography accessible to all.

Blauwbrug

⦿ G6 🏠 **Amstel** 🚊 **14** Ⓜ **Waterlooplein**

The Blauwbrug (Blue Bridge) is thought to have taken its name from the colour of the wooden bridge that originally crossed this particular stretch of the Amstel river in the 17th century. Made of stone, the present light-grey bridge was built in preparation for the 1883 World Colonial Exhibition, which attracted thousands of visitors to Amsterdam. Exhibitors came from 28 different nations.

The Blauwbrug is decorated with sculptures of medieval boats, fish and the imperial crown of Amsterdam and is surmounted by ornate lamps. The design was inspired by the plans for the elaborate Alexander III bridge in Paris.

Amstelkerk

⦿ G7 🏠 **Amstelveld 10** 📞 **520 0060** 🚊 **4** 🕐 **9am–5pm Mon–Fri** 📅 **Public hols**

Designed by Daniel Stalpaert in 1668, the squat and wooden Amstelkerk was originally built as a

> **The real reason to head to Albert Cuypstraat is for its mouthwatering street food. The sound of frying fills the air and your nose will be assaulted by the scents of dishes from around the globe.**

temporary structure, while in the meantime money was going to be raised for a large new church that would be located on the Botermarkt (now Rembrandtplein). Unfortunately, the necessary funds for the grand scheme were never forthcoming, and so the temporary Amstelkerk had to be kept and maintained.

In 1825, the Protestant church authorities attempted to raise money to at least renovate the Amstelkerk's plain interior in a Neo-Gothic style. It was not until 1840, however, when Frederica Elisabeth Cramer donated 25,000 guilders to the project, that work could begin.

During the late 1980s, the Amstelkerk underwent a substantial conversion, which cost some 4 million guilders. Glass-walled offices were installed

←

Outdoor exhibition by the Foam Museum

inside the building and it was closed to the public. However, concerts are still held in the nave, which was preserved in all its Neo-Gothic magnificence. The top-class brasserie NeL is housed in a side building.

Albert Cuypmarkt

📍 F9 **🚇** Albert Cuypstraat **🚊** 3, 4, 12, 24 **Ⓜ** De Pijp **🕐** 9:30am-5pm Mon-Sat **🌐** albertcuypmarkt.amsterdam

The market running along De Pijp's Albert Cuypstraat began trading in 1904, shortly after the expansion of the city. The wide street, once a canal, is named after the Dutch landscape painter Albert Cuyp (1620–91).

This wide street is lined with colour-popping stalls. Described by the stallholders as "the best-known market in Europe", it attracts some 20,000 visitors on weekdays and often twice as many on Saturdays. Vendors sell everything you would expect from a Dutch market – fresh fish, poultry, cheese, fruit and clothes – but the real reason to head to Albert Cuypstraat is for its mouthwatering street food. The sound of frying fills the air and your nose will be assaulted by the scents of dishes from around the globe.

EAT

Café de Punt
Come here for sandwiches made with local cheeses and ham.

📍 G9 **🏠** Tweede Jacob van Campenstraat 150 **🌐** cafe-depunt.nl

€€€

Restaurant de Waaghals
This organic vegetarian restaurant serves imaginative dishes.

📍 E9 **🏠** Franshalsstraat 29 **🕐** L **🌐** waaghals.nl

€€€

Vlaardingse Haringhandel
Locals rate the creamy raw herring served here, in a bun with pickles and onions.

📍 E9 **🏠** Albert Cuypstraat 89 **🕐** Sun & D

€€€

Magere Brug

⊙G7 ⓐAmstel 🚊4

Of Amsterdam's 1,200 or so bridges, the Magere Brug (Skinny Bridge) is undoubtedly the city's best known. The original drawbridge was constructed in about 1670. The traditional story has it that it was named after two sisters called Mager, who lived on either side of the Amstel. However, it appears more likely that the bridge acquired the name from its narrow *(mager)* design. At night many lights illuminate the bridge. The drawbridge was widened in 1871 and most recently rebuilt in 1934, though it still conforms to the traditional double-leaf style. The bridge is made from African azobe wood, and was intended to last for at least 50 years. In 1929, the city council considered whether to demolish the old frame, which had rotted. After huge outcry, it was decided to keep the original.

Since 2003 traffic has been limited to bicycles and pedestrians. Several times a day, the bridge master lets boats through the Magere Brug, then jumps on his bicycle and opens up the Nieuwe Herengracht bridge.

Pathé Tuschinski

⊙F6 ⓐReguliersbree-straat 26-28 📞0900 1458 🚊14, 24 Ⓜ Rokin ⊙Box office: 12:15-10pm daily

Abraham Tuschinski's cinema and variety theatre caused a sensation when it

---

HOW THE MAGERE BRUG WORKS

The Magere Brug is a double-leaf-style drawbridge. This means that it continuously balances its span of 5 m (16 ft) on each side throughout its swing. The balance is made up of two counterweighted beams The arched wooden portal provides a pivot for the balance and a mechanical chain drive operates the steel cables that cause the bridge to lift up.

↑ Magere Brug is illuminated at night by strings of lights

💬 INSIDER TIP
Watch a Film at Pathé Tuschinski

A guided tour of the theatre is certainly recommended, but the best way to appreciate the full opulence of the Pathé Tuschinski is to go to see a film.

designed by Heyman Louis de Jong and decorated by Chris Bartels, Jaap Gidding and Pieter den Besten. In its heyday, Marlene Dietrich and Judy Garland performed here. Now converted into a six-screen cinema, the building has been meticulously restored, both inside and out. The carpet in the entrance hall, replaced in 1984, is an exact copy of the original. For just a few extra euros, you can take a seat in one of the exotic boxes that make up the back row of the huge semicircular, 1,472-seater main auditorium.

opened in 1921. Until then, Amsterdam's cinemas had been sombre places, but this building was an exotic blend of Art Deco and Amsterdam School architecture. Its twin towers are 26 m (85 ft) in height. Built in a slum area known as the Duivelshoek (Devil's Corner), the theatre was

The ornate façade of the Pathé Tuschinski ↑

Stadsarchief Amsterdam

⚐ F7 ⌂ Vijzelstraat 32
🚃 24 🕐 10am–5pm
Tue–Fri, noon–5pm Sat
& Sun 🚫 Public hols
🌐 amsterdam.nl/
stadsarchief

The Stadsarchief, which houses the city's municipal archives, has moved from its former location in Amsteldijk to this monumental building. Designed by K P C de Bazel, who was one of the principal representatives of the Amsterdam School, the edifice was completed in 1926 for the Netherlands Trading Company.

In spite of multiple renovation works, the building retains many attractive original features, such as the colourful floor mosaics (designed by De Bazel himself) and the wooden panelling in the boardrooms on the second floor. There is a permanent display of treasures from the archives in the building's monumental vaults.

In 1991 the building, which is affectionately known as "The Bazel", was declared a national monument. Guided tours take place at 2pm on weekends.

Bloemenmarkt

⚐ F6 ⌂ Singel
🚃 4, 14, 24 Ⓜ Rokin
🕐 9:30am–5pm
daily

On the Singel, west of Muntplein, is the last of the city's floating markets. In the past, nurserymen sailed up the Amstel from their smallholdings and moored here to sell cut flowers and plants directly from their boats. Today, the stalls are still floating but are now a permanent fixture. Despite the sellers' tendency to cater purely for tourists, with prices reflecting this, the displays of fragrant seasonal flowers and bright spring bedding plants are always beautiful to look at.

Museum Van Loon

⚐ F7 ⌂ Keizersgracht
672 🚃 24 Ⓜ Vijzelgracht
🕐 10am–5pm daily
🚫 1 Jan, 27 Apr,
25 Dec 🌐 museum
vanloon.nl

Designed by Adriaan Dortsman, No 672 Keizersgracht is one of a pair of symmetrical houses built

A row of floating
↓ stalls at the
Bloemenmarkt

in 1672. The first resident was the painter Ferdinand Bol, a pupil of Rembrandt. In 1884, the Van Loon family moved into the house. The Van Loons were one of Amsterdam's foremost families in the 17th century.

The house was opened as a museum in 1973, after many years of restoration, retaining the original charming character of the house. It contains a collection of Van Loon family portraits, stretching back to the early 1600s. The period rooms are adorned with fine pieces of furniture, porcelain and sculpture. Some of the upstairs rooms contain sumptuous illusionistic wall paintings, popular in the 17th and 18th centuries. Four were painted by the Classicist artist Gérard de Lairesse (1641–1711).

Outside, in the formal rose garden, is the 18th-century coach house, housing the Van Loon family coaches and livery worn by the servants.

→

Beer wagon displayed at the Heineken Experience

Heineken Experience

📍 F9 🏠 Stadhouderskade 78 🚋 1, 7, 19, 24 Ⓜ Vijzelgracht 🕐 Sep-Jun: 10:30am-7:30pm Mon-Thu, to 9pm Fri-Sun; Jul & Aug: 10:30am-9pm daily; last tickets 2 hours before closing 🌐 heineken experience.com

Gerard Adriaan Heineken founded the Heineken company in 1864 when he bought the 16th-century Hooiberg (haystack) brewery on the Nieuwezijds Voorburgwal. The original Stadhouderskade building was erected in 1867. His readiness to adapt to new methods and bring in foreign brewers established him as a major force in Amsterdam's profitable beer industry. In 1988, the company finally stopped producing beer in its massive brick brewery on Stadhouderskade, as it was unable to keep up with the demand. Production is now concentrated in two breweries, one in Zoeterwoude, near Den Haag, another in Den Bosch. Today, Heineken produces around half of the beer sold in Amsterdam, has production facilities in dozens of countries and exports all over the world.

The Stadhouderskade building now houses the Heineken Experience, where visitors can learn about the history of the company and beer-making in general, and enjoy a free tasting. Extensive renovations accommodate the increasing number of visitors.

There is also a tasting bar, mini brewery and a stable offering the opportunity to view Heineken's splendid dray horses – you may be lucky enough to see them trotting around Amsterdam. Visitors under the age of 18 must be accompanied by an adult.

TULIP MANIA

Tulip mania seized Amsterdam in the 1630s. The exotic Asian bulbs tempted investors and their value soared. At the height of the craze, a single rare bulb could cost more than 10,000 guilders – as much as a grand canalside townhouse. Tempted by the chance to get rich quick, even ordinary folk invested their savings in the flowers, only to lose them when the bubble inevitably burst and prices collapsed in 1637.

A SHORT WALK
AMSTELVELD

Distance 2 km (1.5 miles) **Nearest metro** Waterlooplein **Time** 20 minutes

The eastern end of the Grachtengordel is quiet and largely residential, especially around the Amstelveld, with its pretty wooden church and houseboats. A short walk will take you past shops and numerous cafés, particularly on the bustling Rembrandtplein. As you wander down the broad sweep of the Amstel river, Amsterdam suddenly loses its village atmosphere and begins to feel like a city.

Looking on to the former Botermarkt (butter market) and the cast-iron statue of Rembrandt in Rembrandtplein are dozens of cafés dating from the 19th century, including the De Kroon at No 17.

Café Schiller

↑ Magere Brug, lit up in the evening

| 0 metres | 100 |
| 0 yards | 100 |

N

Did You Know?

The statue of Rembrandt on Rembrantplein is the city's oldest sculpture in a public place.

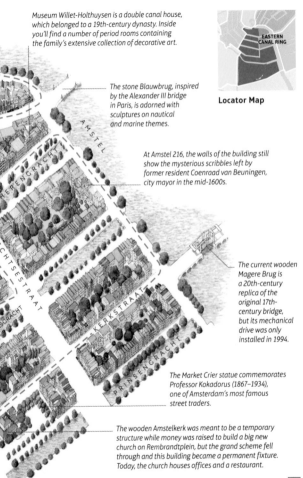

Museum Willet-Holthuysen is a double canal house, which belonged to a 19th-century dynasty. Inside you'll find a number of period rooms containing the family's extensive collection of decorative art.

EASTERN CANAL RING

Locator Map

The stone Blauwbrug, inspired by the Alexander III bridge in Paris, is adorned with sculptures on nautical and marine themes.

At Amstel 216, the walls of the building still show the mysterious scribbles left by former resident Coenraad van Beuningen, city mayor in the mid-1600s.

The current wooden Magere Brug is a 20th-century replica of the original 17th-century bridge, but its mechanical drive was only installed in 1994.

The Market Crier statue commemorates Professor Kokadorus (1867–1934), one of Amsterdam's most famous street traders.

The wooden Amstelkerk was meant to be a temporary structure while money was raised to build a big new church on Rembrandtplein, but the grand scheme fell through and this building became a permanent fixture. Today, the church houses offices and a restaurant.

JORDAAN AND THE WESTERN ISLANDS

Gentrification has taken over much of the once-raffish Jordaan. Old-style taverns are now almost outnumbered by chic boutiques and galleries. As a result, bohemian-minded artists, artisans and performers now favour the streets around Westerpark. Despite the chiming of Westerkerk's bells, the atmosphere here is more hedonistic than holy, with dozens of bars, cafés, galleries and eateries satisfying every desire of a hip clientele.

A red-shuttered building on Prinseneiland, the Western Islands

The cosy lounge, ↑
Houseboat Museum

EXPERIENCE

Houseboat Museum

📍 D5 🏠 Prinsengracht, opposite No 296 🚊 5, 7, 17, 19 🕐 Jan–Jun & Sep–Dec: 10am–5pm Tue–Sun; Jul & Aug: 10am–5pm daily 🚫 1 & 8–24 Jan, 27 Apr, 1st Sat Aug, 25 Dec 🌐 houseboatmuseum.nl

Houseboats line the canals of Amsterdam, homes to people who prefer the alternative lifestyle of being afloat. Moored on the Prinsengracht canal on the edge of the Jordaan, the *Hendrika Maria* is a showcase of life aboard an Amsterdam houseboat. Built in 1914, it served as a barge and transported coal, sand and gravel until the 1960s, when it was converted into a houseboat. It is now the world's only houseboat museum. When inside, visitors can make themselves at home. Note the tiny original kitchen with its green-enamel pots and pans, a hand-pump for water and cosy cupboard-beds, and then take a seat in the surprisingly spacious living room, furnished in chintzy 1950s style, where coffee is served.

Claes Claeszhofje

📍 D3 🏠 1e Eerste Egelantiersdwarsstraat 🚊 5, 13, 17 🕐 Occasionally

This is a group of *hofjes*, the earliest of which was founded in 1616 by a textile merchant, Claes Claesz Anslo. Rescued from ruin in the 1960s by the Stichting Diogenes Foundation, the two sets of houses that comprise this *hofje* are now student lodgings. The houses are set around a pretty little courtyard. One of the oldest surviving and most distinctive is the "Huis met de Schrijvende Hand" (house with the writing hand), at Egelantiersstraat 52. Once the home of a teacher, it dates from the 1630s.

DUTCH HOFJES

Before the Alteration, the Catholic Church usually provided subsidized housing for the poor and elderly, particularly women. During the 17th and 18th centuries, rich merchants and Protestant organizations took on this charitable role and built hundreds of almshouse complexes. Known as *hofjes*, these groups of pretty houses were planned around courtyards or gardens. By providing housing for the elderly and infirm, the *hofjes* marked the beginning of the Dutch welfare system. Visitors are admitted to some but are asked to respect the residents' privacy. Many *hofjes* are found in the Jordaan and some still serve their original purpose.

Zon's Hofje

📍E3 🏠Prinsengracht 159-171 🚋3, 5, 7, 17, 18, 21, 22 🕙10am-5pm Mon-Fri

Until it was turned into almshouses for elderly Mennonite widows, this was the site of a clandestine church. The Kleine Zon (little sun) was a splinter group of the Noah's Ark congregation. Look for the carved sun *(zon)* under the 1765 clock in the courtyard.

De Star Hofje

📍E3 🏠Prinsengracht 89-133 🚋3, 5, 13, 17, 18, 21, 22 🕙6am-6pm Mon-Fri, 6am-2pm Sat

De Star Hofje's lovely flower garden makes it one of the prettiest of the district's *hofjes*, and unique lanterns with a royal crown on each add to the charm. The *hofje* consists of a courtyard surrounded on three sides by houses with a water pump in the middle.

It gets its name from the Star Brewery, which stood here until the *hofje* was built in 1804. Officially known as Van Brienen Hofje, legend has it that a merchant, Jan van Brienen, founded this almshouse in gratitude for his release from a vault in which he had been accidentally imprisoned. Since 1995, it has been owned by a housing foundation.

Noorderkerk

📍E2 🏠Noordermarkt 44-48 🚋3, 5, 13, 17 🚌18, 21, 22 🕙10:30am-12:30pm Mon, 11am-1pm Sat 🌐noorderkerk.org

Built for poor settlers in the Jordaan, the North Church was the first in Amsterdam to be constructed in the shape of a Greek cross. Its layout around a central pulpit allowed all in the encircling pews to see and hear well.

The church was designed by Hendrick de Keyser, who died in 1621, a year before building began. It was completed in 1623. The church is still well

attended by a Calvinist congregation, and bears many reminders of the working-class origins of the Jordaan. By the entrance is a sculpture of three bound figures, inscribed: "Unity is Strength". It commemorates the Jordaanoproer (Jordaan Riot) of 1934 over a reduction in social security. On the south façade is a plaque recalling the strike of February 1941, a protest at the Nazis' deportation of Jews. There are regular concerts held on Saturday afternoons.

Westerpark

📍C1 🏠 Polonceaukade
🚋5 🚌 21, 22, 48, 248
🕐 Museum Het Schip:
11am–5pm Tue–Sun
🌐 westergasfabriek.com
🌐 hetschip.nl

The wasteland that surrounds Amsterdam's former gasworks (Westergasfabriek) was transformed into a 14-ha (35-acre) green park in the early 2000s. Facilities include playgrounds, bars, restaurants, several performance spaces and the Ketelhuis cinema. The gasworks itself has been redeveloped and is being rented out to various associations

↑ Relaxing under Westerpark's blossom

that organize music and food festivals, a variety of performances and exhibitions. Nearby is Het Schip (The Ship), one of the most iconic buildings by the Amsterdam School. Designed by Michel de Klerk in 1919, this apartment block contains 102 homes and the Museum Het Schip, displaying a restored working-class house.

Haarlemmerpoort

📍D1 🏠 Haarlemmerplein
50 🚋 3, 18, 21, 22
🚫 To the public

Originally a defended gateway into Amsterdam, the Haarlemmerpoort marked the beginning of the busy route to Haarlem. The current gateway, dating from 1840, was built for King William II's triumphal entry into the city and officially named Willemspoort. However as the third gateway to be built on or close to this site, it is still known as the

Haarlemmerpoort by Amsterdammers. Designed by Cornelis Alewijn (1788–1839), the Neo-Classical gatehouse was used as tax offices in the 19th century and was made into flats in 1986. Traffic no longer goes through the gate, since a bridge has been built over the adjoining Westerkanaal.

Beyond the Haarlemmerpoort is the peaceful Westerpark, a pleasant retreat.

Pianola en Piano Museum

📍D3 🏠 Westerstraat
106 🚋 3, 5, 13, 17
🕐 11am–5pm Sun & for concerts 🌐 pianola.nl

Fifteen instruments and some 15,000 piano rolls are on show here, celebrating the automatic pianos that were introduced in 1900. There are regular performances by pianists. Sadly, the museum faces closure as it might lose city council subsidies.

←

De Star Hofje's beautiful garden

PLANTAGE

East of the Amstel, this immaculately planned peninsula of tree-lined avenues and gracious 19th-century buildings contrasts with the cramped streets of Oude Zijde, which is only a block or two away. At its centre are the green spaces of Artis – the city's zoo – and Hortus Botanicus Amsterdam, which kids will love exploring. On the gentrified Entrepotdok waterfront, centuries-old warehouses have been turned into upscale apartments. Where the waters of the Nieuwevaart and the Oosterdok meet, a flotilla of historic ships lies at anchor.

The verdant Oosterpark, with its tranquil lake ↓

The museum, with the *Amsterdam* moored outside, and "Tale of the Whale" in the West wing *(inset)* ↑

HET SCHEEPVAARTMUSEUM

📍 K5 🏛 Kattenburgerplein 1 🚌 22, 48 🚇 Nemo 🕐 9am–5pm daily ⛔ 1 Jan, 27 Apr, 25 Dec 🌐 hetscheepvaartmuseum.nl

Once the arsenal of the Amsterdam Admiralty, this vast Classical sandstone building was constructed by Daniel Stalpaert in 1656 around a massive courtyard. The admiralty stayed in residence until 1973, when the building was converted into the Maritime Museum. The artillery courtyard now has a glass roof.

Visitors of all ages enjoy the museum's interactive exhibitions and displays of maritime objects. Don't miss the free audio tour. The open courtyard gives access to the three wings of the building, each with its own theme. Oost (East) has displays of maritime objects, paintings, globes and model yachts. In Noord (North), visitors can take a journey back to the Dutch Golden Age using the latest virtual reality technology. Climb aboard the East Indiaman *Amsterdam*: haul up cargo, crawl through the hold and even fire a cannon. The West wing has interactive exhibits geared towards children, such as "Tale of the Whale".

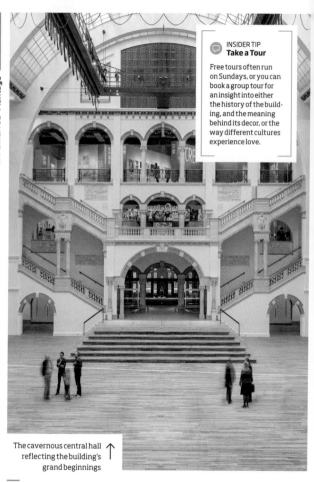

The cavernous central hall reflecting the building's grand beginnings ↑

TROPENMUSEUM

📍 L7 🏠 Linnaeusstraat 2 🚋 7, 14, 19 🕐 10am–5pm Tue–Sun (daily during school hols) ⊘ 1 Jan, 27 Apr, 25 Dec 🌐 tropenmuseum.nl

This fascinating museum reflects the Netherlands' colonial history, as well as the diversity of the country today. The displays of art objects, photographs and film focus on widely different cultures in the tropics and subtropics. Children will love the interactive Tropenmuseum Junior.

The Main Collection

Built to house the Dutch Colonial Institute, this vast complex was finished in 1926 by architects M A and J J Nieukerken. The exterior of what is one of the city's finest historic buildings is decorated with symbols of imperialism, such as stone friezes of peasants planting rice.

In 1978, the Royal Tropical Institute opened this fascinating ethnographic museum. One floor holds treasures from Indonesia, Papua New Guinea and Southeast Asia. The collection aims to

↑ The museum's exterior, made from red brick

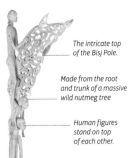

The intricate top of the Bisj Pole.

Made from the root and trunk of a massive wild nutmeg tree

Human figures stand on top of each other.

← Carved to satisfy the spirits of cannibalized men, the Bisj Pole – a ritual totem from New Guinea

show the things that unite all cultures, from love to death. On the upper floors, the exhibitions use static and interactive displays to explore diverse topics, including body art and Afrofuturism. Temporary exhibitions are held in the North Wing on the ground floor and the Park Hall on the second floor.

Tropenmuseum Junior

The museum espouses the importance of children learning about different cultures. This immersive Dutch exhibition allows kids to see, hear, smell and taste what it's like to live in a different country. The destination changes every two and a half years. Until early 2020, youngsters board a simulated plane bound for Morocco. Once they've met their guides, they'll experience aspects of Moroccan life.

De Gooyer windmill, a
quintessentially Dutch image

EXPERIENCE MORE

De Gooyer Windmill

⊙ M6 **⌂** Funenkade 5
🚊 7, 14 **🚌** 22 **🔒** To
the public

Of the six remaining
windmills within the city's
boundaries, De Gooyer, also
known as the Funenmolen,
is the most central. Dominating the view down the
Nieuwevaart, the mill was
built around 1725, and was
the first cornmill in the
Netherlands to use
streamlined sails.

It first stood to the west
of its present site, but the
Oranje Nassau barracks,
built in 1814, acted as a
windbreak, and the mill
was then moved to the
Funenkade. The octagonal
wooden structure was
rebuilt on the stone footings
of an earlier water-pumping
mill, demolished in 1812.

By 1925, De Gooyer was in
a very poor state of repair
and was bought by the
city council, which fully
restored it. Since then, the
lower part of the mill, with
its neat thatched roof and
tiny windows, has been a
private home, though its
massive sails still creak
into action sometimes.
Next to the mill is the
Brouwerij Het IJ, one of
two independent
breweries in the city.

10,000

windmills once
dotted the Dutch
landscape.

Hollandsche Schouwburg

⊙ J6 **⌂** Plantage
Middenlaan 24 **🚊** 14
🕐 11am–5pm daily **🔒** 27
Apr, Rosh Hashanah
(Jewish New Year), Yom
Kippur **🌐** jck.nl/en

Part of the Jewish Cultural
Quarter, this former
theatre is now a memorial
to the 104,000 Dutch
Jewish victims of World
War II. Thousands were
detained here before
being deported to
concentration camps.
Postwar, the building
was abandoned until 1962.
A basalt column with a
base in the shape of the
Star of David now stands
on the site of the stage.
Written behind it is: "To
the memory of those
taken from here." Follow-
ing its restoration in 1993,
the building became an
education centre. On the

ground floor, a candle illuminates the names of the war victims. Upstairs, there is a touching permanent exhibition on the persecution of the Jews in the Netherlands from 1940 to 1945.

Hortus Botanicus Amsterdam

📍 J6 🏛 Plantage Middenlaan 2 🚊 9, 14 Ⓜ Waterlooplein 🕙 10am–5pm daily 🚫 1 Jan, 25 Dec 🌐 dehortus.nl

Beginning life as a small apothecary's herb garden in 1682, this green oasis in the centre of Amsterdam now boasts one of the world's largest botanical collections. Its range of flora expanded when tropical plants were brought back by the Dutch East India Company. In 1706, it became the first place outside Arabia to succeed in cultivating the coffee plant.

The medicinal herb garden has several species of plants that were available in the 17th century and are of great importance to medicine, such as *Acorus calamus*. The glass-domed Palm House, built in 1912, contains a collection of palms, conservatory plants and cycads, including one that is more than 400 years old. The restored orangery has a

café and terrace, where art shows with a botanical theme are held.

A modern glass-and-aluminium construction, designed by Moshé Zwarts and Rein Jansma, was opened in 1993 to make room for the tropical, subtropical and desert plants. There is also a butterfly house, with many species flying around, and a shop where you can purchase plants and gardening tools.

Muziekgebouw aan 't IJ

📍 K3 🏛 Piet Heinkade 1 🚊 26 🌐 muziekge bouw.nl

A huge glass box that juts into the IJ, this spectacular concert hall opened in 2005. Sharing its complex with the BIMHUIS, Amsterdam's leading jazz venue, Muziekgebouw aan 't IJ is versatile. It is capable of hosting both intimate chamber-music performances and large-scale concerts, with standing room for audiences of up to 1,500 people. As well as classical music, it presents performances of everything from electro to world music. The building also runs an annual programme of contemporary art and photography exhibitions. Order tickets for the coming season online before 1 October for discounts of 20 to 35 per cent.

EAT

Café Restaurant Plantage

Dine in the leafy courtyard.

📍 J6 🏛 Plantage Kerklaan 36 🌐 caferestaurantde plantage.nl

Restaurant Stalpaert

Het Scheepvaartmuseum's café offers snacks and soups.

📍 K5 🏛 Kattenburgerplein 1 🌐 hetscheepvaart museum.com

Bloem Eten en Drinken

Organic dishes are served on Bloem's waterside terrace.

📍 K5 🏛 Entrepotdok 36 🚫 Mon 🌐 bloem36.nl

Hermitage Amsterdam

📍 H7 🏛 Amstel 51
🚊 4, 14 Ⓜ Waterlooplein
🚌 City Hall 🕐 10am–5pm daily 🗓 27 Apr
🌐 hermitage.nl

The State Hermitage Museum in St Petersburg, Russia, decided upon Amsterdam as the ideal city in which to open an international satellite branch, which would display rotating temp-orary exhibitions drawn from the Hermitage's rich and extensive collection.

The Hermitage Amsterdam opened in early 2004, in a side wing of the Amstelhof (a former old people's home), with a spectacular exhibition of fine Greek gold jewellery from the 6th to the 2nd centuries BC. Other exhibitions have included the collection of the last Tsars Nicholas and Alexandra, and the Portrait Gallery of the Golden Age. The Amstelhof building, which stands in a stunning position overlooking the Amstel river, has been fully restored.

The Hermitage Amsterdam has taken over the whole complex, with two exhibition wings, an auditorium and a children's wing where youngsters can discover their own creative talents.

There is also a lovely café-restaurant on the first floor where visitors can enjoy an invigorating cup of tea or coffee, a tasty lunch or a refreshing glass of wine.

Museum 't Kromhout

📍 L6 🏛 Hoogte Kadijk 147 🚊 7, 14 🚌 22
🕐 9:30am–3:30pm Tue & 3rd Sun of month
🌐 kromhoutmuseum.nl

The Museum 't Kromhout is one of the oldest working shipyards in Amsterdam. Ships were built here as early as 1757. As ocean-going ships got bigger in the second half of the 19th century due to industrial developments, the yard, due to its small size, turned to building lighter craft for inland waterways. It is now used only for restoration and repair work. The museum is dedicated to the history of marine engineering, with engines, maritime photographs and a well-equipped, original forge.

Entrepotdok

🔲 K6 🚊 14 🚌 22

The redevelopment of the old VOC warehouses at Entrepotdok has revitalized this dockland area. It was the greatest warehouse area in Europe during the mid-19th century, being a customs-free zone for goods in transit. The quayside buildings of Entrepotdok are now a lively complex of offices, homes and eating places. Some of the original façades of the warehouses have been preserved, unlike the interiors, which have been opened up to provide an attractive inner courtyard. Café tables are often set out alongside the canal. On the other side, coloured houseboats are moored side by side, and herons doze at the water's edge.

Verzetsmuseum

🔲 J6 🅰 Plantage Kerklaan 61 🚊 14
🕐 10am-5pm Mon-Fri, 11am-5pm Sat, Sun & public hols 🗓 1 Jan, 27 Apr, 25 Dec
🌐 verzetsmuseum.org

Located in a building that used to be the home of

← Portrait Gallery of the Golden Age, Hermitage Amsterdam

↑ Resistance posters and memorabilia on display in the Verzetsmuseum

a Jewish choral society, the Resistance Museum holds a fascinating collection of memorabilia recording the activities of Dutch Resistance workers in World War II. It focuses on the courage of the 25,000 people actively involved in the movement. On display are false documents, film clips, slide shows, photographs, weaponry, equipment and personal items belonging to the workers.

By 1945 there were over 300,000 people in hiding in the Netherlands, including Jews and anti-Nazi Dutch. Subsequent events organized by the Resistance, like the dockers' strike against the deportation of the Jews, are brought to life by exhibits showing where the refugees hid and how food was smuggled in. The museum includes a special children's wing,

Verzetsmuseum Junior, in which the real-life wartime experiences of children are told. The story begins via a time machine that transports visitors back to the 1940s.

A SHORT WALK
PLANTAGE

Distance 2.5 km (1.5 miles) **Nearest tram** 9, 14 (Artis) **Time** 25 minutes

With its wide, tree-lined streets and painted, sandstone buildings, the Plantage is a graceful and often overlooked part of the city. Though it seems like a quiet part of town, there is a lot to see and do, with a diverse range of popular attractions which can get very busy on sunny days. The area, which is dominated by the Artis complex, has a strong Jewish tradition, and several monuments commemorate Jewish history in Amsterdam, including a basalt memorial in the Hollandsche Schouwburg. The cafés of the Entrepotdok offer a pleasant setting for a relaxing coffee, within earshot of the zoo.

Inspired by an Italian palazzo, De Burcht was the headquarters of the Dutch Diamond Workers' Union.

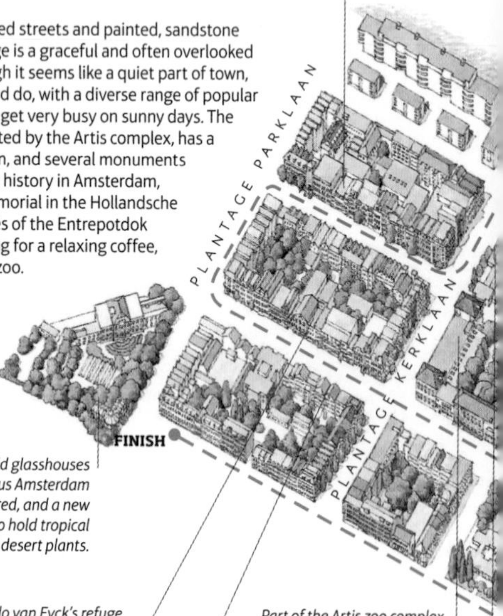

PLANTAGE PARKLAAN

PLANTAGE KERKLAAN

FINISH

The old glasshouses at Hortus Botanicus Amsterdam have been restored, and a new one erected to hold tropical and desert plants.

Moederhuis – Aldo van Eyck's refuge for pregnant women – has a colourful, modern façade intended to draw people inside.

Little remains of the Hollandsche Schouwburg, a former theatre which is now a sombre monument to the deported Jews of World War II.

Part of the Artis zoo complex, Micropia is the world's first museum dedicated to microbes and micro-organisms, with cutting-edge displays.

The domed Planetarium explores man's relationship with the stars. Interactive displays show the positions of the planets.

Entrepotdok was the largest warehouse development in Europe during the 19th century. It has been redeveloped and transformed into an attractive quayside housing, office and leisure complex.

Locator Map

START

More than 900 species, including a pride of lions, live in the Artis zoo complex, which occupies a beautifully laid-out garden site.

→

Entrepotdok, formerly warehouses, sitting on the water

Artis restaurant

PLANTAGE MIDDENLAAN

The historic building that once stood here has been demolished and the new one is under construction.

0 metres 100

0 yards 100

N ↑

NOORD

This edgy neighbourhood is a five-minute ferry ride across the IJ from the city centre. Noord is a rejuvenated dockland with a youthful, post-industrial vibe. Former factories and warehouses have been transformed into performance venues, ateliers and galleries, eateries and boutique hotels. Street art enlivens once-derelict buildings, flea markets take over formerly sleepy streets and locals lounge on deckchairs on a man-made beach. The 100-m- (328-ft-) high A'DAM Toren, with its trendy clubs and revolving restaurant, is the district's emblematic landmark of transformation.

↓ The graphic exterior of EYE

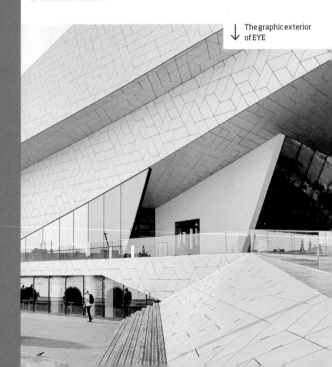

A'DAM TOREN

📍Q14 🏠Overhoeksplein 1 🚊Buiksloterweg 🚌38
🚇Centraal Station 🕐Daily; A'DAM Lookout: 10am–10pm daily 🌐adamtoren.nl

Unlike most cities, Amsterdam's skyline is free of massive skyscrapers, so Amsterdammers look across the River IJ at the 100-m- (328-ft-) high A'DAM Toren with some affection. An icon of the post-industrial Noord, this multi-storey colossus has become the city's most exciting cultural complex.

The 22-storey tower was built for oil giant Royal Dutch Shell in 1971 and acted as the company's headquarters until 2009. Many locals still call it the "Shelltoren" (Shell tower). Reborn in 2016 after a massive refit, it is now packed with places to eat, drink, dance and shop, including Moon, a revolving restaurant, as well as one of the city's classiest hotels – Sir Adam. A high-speed elevator whisks visitors with tickets to A'DAM Lookout, on the 21st floor, which offers an unbeatable 360-degree view of Amsterdam. This is the perfect vantage point for photographers, particularly at sunset. Thrill-seekers, unsatisfied by the observation deck alone, can soar 100 m (328 ft) above the city on "Over the Edge", a two-seater swing.

Did You Know?

"Over the Edge" is the highest swing in Europe.

A'DAM Toren dominating the skyline of Noord and overlooking the River IJ

TOP 5 A'DAM TOREN SPACES

A'DAM Lookout
Enjoy a cocktail at the rooftop bar or swing over the city.

Moon
This restaurant revolves to give diners unbeatable views.

Sir Adam
A cool, boutique hotel, offering guests floor-to-ceiling windows, espresso machines and a pillow menu.

Shelter
Contemporary art and dance music make up the programme of events at this club.

Madam
This bar and eatery is on the 20th floor.

EXPERIENCE MORE

NDSM

📍 P11 🏠 Neveritaweg 61
🌐 ndsm.nl

The giant factory building at the heart of the former NDSM shipyard (on the banks of the River IJ) has become the core of Amsterdam's most vibrant cultural quarter. Some of the city's hottest young creative talents live and work here in spaces created from vintage shipping containers. Those wanting to find out about NDSM's history and future can take a guided tour of the complex and meet some of the "city nomads" who make this area buzz.

Crammed with quirky shops and craft studios, bars, cafés, restaurants and nightspots, the complex also attracts visitors with its festivals, dance events and exhibitions. It even has its own artificial beach – Pllek – where city slickers sunbathe, practise yoga and listen to live music. In the summer months, Sun-screenings takes over the beach for its packed open-air cinema season.

It seems appropriate that this colourful area became the home of the world's largest street-art museum in late 2019. Lasloods, NDSM's cavernous former welding hangar, has been transformed by specially commissioned works created by street-art superstars from around the world. Don't miss Brazilian Eduardo Kobra's huge mural of Anne Frank, *Let Me Be Myself* on the exterior of the building. The artist used 500 cans of spray paint and 40 litres of gloss to complete the 240-sq-m (2,583-sq-ft) work.

Pekmarkt

📍 R13 🏠 Van der Pekstraat
🚇 Buiksloterweg
🕐 11am–5pm Wed, Fri & Sat 🌐 pekmarkt.nl

Three days a week, Van der Pekstraat comes alive as a farmers' market. Dozens of stalls sell all manner of goods, including craft cheeses, artisan breads and sizzling sausages.

For visitors, the best day to come is Saturday, when art, vintage clothing and quirky fashion accessories are on sale alongside food and drink.

EYE

📍 Q14 🏠 IJpromenade 1
🚇 Buiksloterweg
🎟 Ticket office: 10am–10pm daily; exhibitions: 11am–5pm daily
🌐 eyefilm.nl/en

Located on the northern bank of the River IJ, the EYE is a merger between

the Filmmuseum, housed for almost 40 years in what is now VondelCS, and several other Dutch cine-matic organizations. The museum's huge collection tells the story of the Netherlands film industry, from silent films at the end of the 19th century to advances in digital technology and 3D cinema today. There is also a wide display of movie memorabilia, including photographs, soundtracks, technical equipment and posters.

The museum has come a long way from its former 19th-century home in a park's pavilion. The EYE now occupies a sleek white building that, unsurprisingly, is designed to resemble a giant eye. Inside are four cinemas, an exhibition space and a café-restaurant, with a waterside terrace that offers stunning views across the harbour on sunny days.

In the basement, visitors can watch silent films from the museum's vast collection in specially-designed viewing capsules, with three-seater sofas. A room also plays a 360-degree projection of film

Bicycles parked in front of repurposed shipping containers at NDSM

← All sorts of interesting items for sale at IJ-Hallen

clips. Entrance to the basement is included in the cost of a cinema or exhibition ticket.

IJ-Hallen

P11 ⌂ **TT Neveritaweg 15** 🚇 **NDSM Werf** ⏱ **9am–4:30pm 2nd weekend each month** 🌐 **ijhallen.nl**

For bargain hunters and shopping lovers this flea market is a must. Held in the cavernous IJ-Hallen, it is the largest in Europe. On a busy day, visitors might find as many as 750 stands at this colourful, bustling site. Traders peddle everything from collectable vinyl to vintage clothing from bygone decades. There are also plenty of stalls selling snacks and drinks. Arrive early to find the best stock, but those who arrive later may find the best bargains.

Between April and September the market is held outside, while for the rest of the year it moves indoors into the giant for-mer warehouse building. Look out for the cool graffiti on the walls.

EAT

Restaurant Pllek

In a space created from upcycled shipping containers and other salvaged materials, Pllek is a food-and-drink hot spot.

P11 ⌂ **TT Neveritaweg 59** 🌐 **pllek.nl**

€€€

BEYOND AMSTERDAM

Amsterdam is at the northern edge of a region known as the Randstad, the economic powerhouse of the Netherlands. Within easy reach of the capital are the ancient towns of Leiden and Utrecht, as well as Den Haag and Haarlem with their exceptional galleries and museums. The Randstad extends south as far as Rotterdam, a thriving modern city full of avant-garde architecture.

North of Amsterdam, the traditional fishing communities that once depended on the Zuiderzee, before it was closed off from the sea in 1932, have now turned to tourism for their income. Much of the land here was reclaimed from the sea over the last 300 years, and the fertile soil is farmed intensively. Spreading to the southwest, dazzling colours carpet the fields in spring, and the exquisite gardens at Keukenhof are the showcase of the Dutch bulb industry.

A windmill in
a tulip field in
↓ Noord-Holland

ZUIDERZEEMUSEUM

⌂ Wierdijk, Enkhuizen; 50 km (31 miles) NE of Amsterdam 🚉 Enkhuizen
🚌 Leaves from behind train station (Apr–Oct) ⏱ Indoor museum: 10am–5pm
daily; Open-air museum: 10am–5pm Apr–Oct 🌐 zuiderzeemuseum.nl

**Step back in time at this fascinating open-air museum which recreates
daily life in a traditional fishing village on the Zuiderzee – a bay of the
North Sea – in the early 20th century.**

Enkhuizen was one of several villages around the edge
of the Zuiderzee whose fishing-based economy was
devastated when access to the North Sea was blocked by
construction of the Afsluitdijk dam in 1932. The village's
fortunes were revived with the opening of this museum
complex. The *binnenmuseum* (indoor museum) focuses
on the Zuiderzee history, including an impressive display
of historic boats. The *buitenmuseum* (open-air museum)
consists of rescued buildings, reconstructed to create a
typical Zuiderzee village, with demonstrations of local crafts.

Did You Know?

Herring is preserved
by being smoked
over smouldering
woodchips.

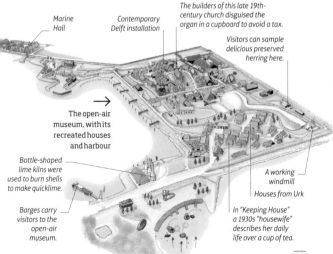

Marine
Hall

Contemporary
Delft installation

The builders of this late 19th-
century church disguised the
organ in a cupboard to avoid a tax.

Visitors can sample
delicious preserved
herring here.

The open-air
museum, with its
recreated houses
and harbour

Bottle-shaped
lime kilns were
used to burn shells
to make quicklime.

Barges carry
visitors to the
open-air
museum.

A working
windmill

Houses from Urk

In "Keeping House"
a 1930s "housewife"
describes her daily
life over a cup of tea.

Cycling through the endless
tulip fields between
Haarlem and Leiden ↑

THE BULBFIELDS

 Haarlem

Occupying a 30-km (19-mile) strip between Haarlem and Leiden, the Bloembollenstreek is the main bulb-growing area in the Netherlands. The most cultivated bulbs in the Netherlands include gladioli, lilies, daffodils, hyacinths, irises, crocuses and dahlias, but tulips are still far and away the country's most popular flower.

When to Go

From late January, the polders (land reclaimed from the sea) bloom with a series of vividly coloured bulbs, beginning with early crocuses and building to a climax around mid-April, when the tulips flower. Late-blooming flowers, such as lilies, extend the season into late May.

Aalsmeer

This town is home to the world's largest flower auction – the Bloemenveiling Royal FloraHolland. As the 12.5 billion cut flowers and pot plants sold here annually all have a short shelf life, speed is of the essence. A reverse auction is held. The price decreases as the big-screen auction clock counts down and buyers stop the clock at any price point. Visitors can watch the proceedings from a viewing gallery above the trading floor.

Keukenhof

Situated on the outskirts of Lisse, this garden was set up in 1949 as a showcase for Dutch bulb growers and is now planted with some 7 million bulbs. Keukenhof is at its most spectacular from late March to late May, when drifts of daffodils, hyacinths or tulips form. Japanese cherry trees shed snowy blossom early in the season, and there are splashes of azaleas and rhododendrons later in the year.

TOP 5

TOP FIVE DUTCH BULBS

Aladdin Tulips
A lily-shaped flower, which has red petals with yellow tips.

China Pink Tulips
Delicate stems are crowned with vibrant pink flowers.

Tahiti Daffodils
Double-formed, golden-yellow petals nestle in a small orange centre.

Minnow Daffodils
A fragrant, miniature daffodil with cream-coloured blooms.

Blue Jacket Hyacinths
Striped petals form a cone of blue flowers, with a heady scent.

↑ Carpets of tulips and grape hyacinths snaking through the Keukenhof gardens

HAARLEM

🏠 20 km (12 miles) W of Amsterdam 🚉 Haarlem
ℹ️ Grote Markt 2; www.haarlemmarketing.nl

A prosperous city in the Golden Age, Haarlem retains much of its 17th-century character, with its brick-paved lanes around the Grote Markt.

Haarlem had grown into a thriving cloth-making centre by the 15th century. Today, the city is the commercial capital of Noord Holland province. It is the centre of the Dutch printing, pharmaceutical and bulb-growing industries, but there is little sign of this in the delightful pedestrianized streets of the historic heart of the city. Most of the sites of interest are within easy walking distance of the Grote Markt, a lively square packed with old buildings, cafés and restaurants. Old bookshops, antique dealers and traditional food shops are all to be discovered in nearby streets.

The Hoofdwacht is a 17th-century former guard house.

The Grote Markt is the bustling centre of the city.

SMEDESTR

BARTELJORISSTRAAT

GROTE MARKT

KONINGSTRAAT

GR HOUTSTR

LEPELSTRAAT

The Vleeshal (1603) – an old meat market – is part of the Frans Hals Museum.

↑ The Teylers Museum's two-storey oval hall was added in 1779, and contains glass cabinets full of bizarre minerals and cases of intimidating medical instruments

Statue of Laurens Jansz Coster (1370–1440) who is believed to have invented printing in 1423, 16 years before Gutenberg.

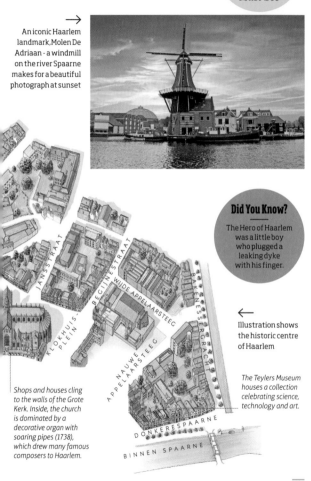

An iconic Haarlem landmark, Molen De Adriaan - a windmill on the river Spaarne makes for a beautiful photograph at sunset

Did You Know?

The Hero of Haarlem was a little boy who plugged a leaking dyke with his finger.

Illustration shows the historic centre of Haarlem

The Teylers Museum houses a collection celebrating science, technology and art.

Shops and houses cling to the walls of the Grote Kerk. Inside, the church is dominated by a decorative organ with soaring pipes (1738), which drew many famous composers to Haarlem.

LEIDEN

🏠 35 km (22 miles) SW of Amsterdam 🚉 Leiden Centraal
ℹ️ Stationsweg 41; www.visitleiden.nl

Leiden is famous for its university, the oldest and most prestigious in the Netherlands. During termtime, the streets are crowded with students cycling between lectures or packing the cafés and bookshops.

The university was founded in 1575 by William of Orange, a year after he relieved the town from a year-long siege by the Spanish. As a reward for their endurance, William offered the citizens of Leiden a choice: the building of a university or the abolition of tax. They chose wisely, and the city's reputation as a centre of intellectual and religious tolerance was firmly established. English Puritan dissidents, victims of persecution in their homeland, were able to settle here in the 17th century before undertaking their epic voyage to the New World. A number of exceptional museums document Leiden's turbulent history, including the 17th-century Golden Age, when the town was a centre for worldwide trade. This age also saw the birth of the city's most famous son – Rembrandt – in June 1606. Look for the wall plaque on the façade of his birthplace on Weddesteeg.

Langebrug is lined with student accommodation.

Rijksmuseum van Oudheden

Hortus Botanicus Leiden

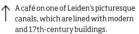

↑ A café on one of Leiden's picturesque canals, which are lined with modern and 17th-century buildings.

↑ Illustration shows the area around Pieterskerk in Leiden

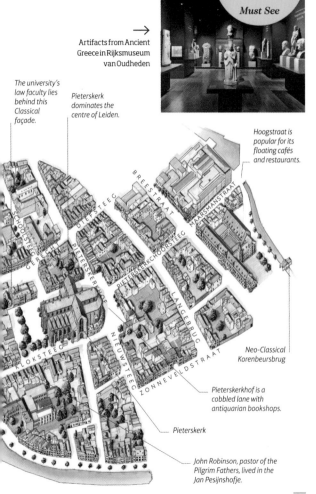

→ Artifacts from Ancient Greece in Rijksmuseum van Oudheden

Must See

The university's law faculty lies behind this Classical façade.

Pieterskerk dominates the centre of Leiden.

Hoogstraat is popular for its floating cafés and restaurants.

SCHOOLSTEEG

GERECHT

DIEFSTEEG

PIETERSKERKHOF

BREESTRAAT

PIETERSKERKCHOORSTEEG

MAARSMANSTRAAT

LANGEBRUG

NIEUWSTEEG

KLOKSTEEG

ZONNEVELDSTRAAT

Neo-Classical Korenbeursbrug

Pieterskerkhof is a cobbled lane with antiquarian bookshops.

Pieterskerk

John Robinson, pastor of the Pilgrim Fathers, lived in the Jan Pesijnshofje.

DELFT

🏠 50 km (31 miles) SW of Amsterdam
🚉 Delft ℹ️ Kerkstraat 3; 🌐 delft.nl

The charming town of Delft is known the world over for its blue-and-white pottery, but it is equally famous as the resting place of William of Orange (1533–84) and as the birthplace of artist Jan Vermeer (1632–75).

The origins of Delft date from 1075 and its prosperity was based on weaving and brewing. An explosion at the national arsenal destroyed much of the medieval town in October 1645 and the centre was rebuilt in the late 17th century. The sleepy old town has changed little since then – gabled Gothic and Renaissance houses still line the tree-shaded canals. Activity centres on the market square, bordered by the Stadhuis and Nieuwe Kerk. Visitors can dip into the scores of shops selling antiques and delftware.

SCHOOLSTRAAT

ST AGATHA PLEIN

OUDE DELFT

NIEUWSTRAAT

OUDE DELFT

→ The centre of Delft, which is illustrated here, boasts two iconic churches

1396 Chapel of St Hippolytus

Oude Delft is lined with Renaissance canal houses

← The magnificent organ, which contains the tombs of eminent Delft citizens.

←

The façade of the Vleeshal - the old meat market - with its animal heads, stands out from the other buildings nearby

INSIDER TIP
Delftware

Instead of buying the famed hand-painted porcelain in the expensive boutiques in the centre of the town, head to a local factory. Their shops are often reasonably priced and you can take a tour.

Stadhuis (1618)

Vleeshal (1650)

Did You Know?

Vermeer's nickname is "The Sphinx of Delft" because so little is known of his life.

ROTTERDAM

🏠 65 km (40 miles) SW of Amsterdam 🚆 Rotterdam Centraal ✈ 6 km (4 miles) NW 🛈 Rotterdam Centraal station and Coolsingel 114; www.rotterdam.info

Rotterdam's ancient heart was ravaged during World War II, due to its prominent port. Much of the city has been rebuilt in experimental styles, resulting in some of Europe's most original and innovative architecture.

Maritiem Museum Rotterdam

🏠 Leuvehaven 1 ⏰ 10am–5pm Tue–Sat, also 11am–5pm Sun & Mon in Jul & Aug 🚫 Public hols 🌐 maritiemmuseum.nl

Rotterdam occupies a strategic maritime position. The city sits where the Rijn (Rhine), Europe's most important river, meets the North Sea and, as a result, has always been a centre for trade. Today, barges from Rotterdam transport goods deep into the continent, and ocean-going ships carry European exports around the world. Rotterdam is therefore a fitting city for a museum dedicated to the historic seafaring prowess of the Netherlands. Prince Hendrik, brother of King William III, founded this museum in 1873. Highlights include the oldest model ship in Europe, a miniature version of one of Columbus's cargo ships. Also worth a visit is the museum harbour, where you can explore artfully restored barges and steamships. Children will love the interactive Professor Splash area where they can play games while learning

Did You Know?

Covering 105 sq km (41 sq miles), Rotterdam is the biggest port in Europe.

← The striking tilting yellow cubes of the Kubuswoningen

about ships and what it's like to work in a port.

Kubuswoningen

🏠 Overblaak 70
🕐 10am–6pm daily
🌐 kubuswoning.nl

Much of Oudehaven, the old harbour area of Rotterdam, was bombed in World War II and it has largely been rebuilt in daring and avant-garde styles. The pencil-shaped apartment block, Blaaktoren, and the adjacent "cube houses", Kubuswoningen, were designed by architect Piet Blom (1934–99), and built in 1982–4. The structuralist buildings were designed to integrate with their surroundings, but also to encourage social inter-action among its occupants. The Kubuswoningen are extraordinary apartments, set on concrete stilts and tilted at a crazy angle. Each cube contains three floors. The lowest floor is a trian-gular living space, with its windows looking down on the street, while the second floor houses the bedrooms and has sky-facing windows. The top floor forms a three-sided pyramid, with 18 windows and 3 hatches,

offering amazing views. Residents have specially designed furniture to fit the sloping rooms.

Euromast

🏠 Parkhaven 20
🕐 Apr–Sep: 9:30am–10pm daily; Oct–Mar: 10am–10pm daily 🌐 euromast.nl

This futuristic structure enjoys sweeping views of Rotterdam. At a height of 100 m (328 ft), the lower section, built in 1960, has a viewing platform with a rest-aurant. In 1970 the Space Tower added another 85 m (279 ft) to the structure to make this the tallest con-struction in the Netherlands. An exterior "space cabin" ascends 58 m (190 ft) from the viewing platform.

Kunsthal

🏠 Westzeedijk 341
🕐 10am–5pm Tue–Sat, 11am–5pm Sun & public hols 🚫 1 Jan, 27 Apr, 25 Dec 🌐 kunsthal.nl

From costume and art to inventions and photography, the Kunsthal delivers exhi-bitions that alternate bet-ween traditional "high art" and pop culture. There is no permanent collection. The eye-catching building was designed in 1998 by Rotterdam's Rem Koolhaas, whose other works include the Beijing headquarters for China Central Television.

His use of materials, such as corrugated plastic, and an orange steel girder that sticks out over the edge of the roof draw attention.

Wereldmuseum Rotterdam

🏠 Willemskade 25 🕐 10am–5pm Tue–Sun 🚫 Public hols 🌐 wereldmuseum.nl

During the 17th century, the city fathers amassed a superb ethnological collec-tion. The Wereldmuseum displays 1,800 artifacts from Indonesia, the Americas and Asia, and presents audio-visual displays of theatre, film, dance and music. The museum reflects 127 of the 170 different nationalities who live in Rotterdam. After exploring the collection, take a break in the café, which offers river views.

EAT

Restaurant de Jong
Chef Jim de Jong's spectacular six-course menu uses local produce.

🏠 Nobelstraat 143
🌐 restaurantde jong.nl

UTRECHT

🏠 57 km (35 miles) SE of Amsterdam   🚉 Hoog Catharijne
ℹ️ Domplein 9; www.visit-utrecht.com

In Utrecht's city centre medieval churches and monasteries stand alongside modern blocks and a vast undercover shopping complex. The Oudegracht (old canal), lined with broad quays, cellar bars and cafés, threads its way through the city.

Domkerk

🏠 Achter de Dom 1
🕐 Daily   🌐 domkerk.nl

Construction of the cathedral began in 1254. Today, only the north and south transepts, two chapels and the choir remain, along with the 15th-century cloisters and a chapterhouse (1495), which is now part of the university. Outside the church is a giant boulder, dated 980 and covered with runic symbols. It was presented to Utrecht by the Danish people in 1936, to commemorate Denmark's early conversion to Christianity by missionaries from Utrecht. The soaring 112-m- (367-ft-)high Domtoren has always stood apart from the cathedral.

Nijntje Museum

🏠 Agnietenstraat 2
🕐 10am–5pm Tue–Sun
🚫 1 Jan, 27 Apr, 25 Dec
🌐 nijntjemuseum.nl

Reserve your ticket online for the always popular Nijntje Museum. It is dedicated to the most famous nijntje (little rabbit) in the Netherlands – Miffy – and her creator, Dick Bruna (1927–2017).

Inside, younger kids can explore ten themed rooms inspired by characters from Bruna's many picture books, listen to story readings, or join a creative workshop. It's a playful learning experience that avoids being either too twee or commercialized.

Must See

↑ A child hugging a Miffy mascot at the Nijntje Museum

Museum Catharijneconvent

🏛 Lange Nieuwstraat 38
🕐 10am–5pm Tue–Fri; from 11am Sat, Sun & public hols 🚫 1 Jan, 27 Apr
🌐 catharijneconvent.nl

The beautiful former convent of St Catherine (1562) is now home to a fascinating museum dealing with the often troubled history of religion in the Netherlands. On the upper floors, a series of model church interiors highlights the changes in religious philosophies through the ages. They range from the lavish statues and paintings in a Catholic church to the more austere, unadorned interiors typical of Protestant churches.

Museum Speelklok

🏛 Buurkerk on Steenweg 6 🕐 10am–5pm Tue–Sun (daily during school hols) 🚫 1 Jan, 27 Apr, 25 Dec 🌐 museums peelklok.nl

This magical place displays a collection of mechanical musical instruments, from the 18th century to the

←

A boat passes a café on one of Utrecht's many canal-side wharfs

present day. Fairground organs compete with music boxes, clocks, carillons, pianolas and automated birds. These instruments are demonstrated on guided tours, during which visitors are encouraged to sing and dance along. The restoration of instruments can be observed in the workshop.

Nederlands Spoorwegmuseum

🏛 Maliebaanstation
🕐 10am–5pm Tue–Sun & public hols (daily during school hols)
🚫 1 Jan, 27 Apr
🌐 spoorwegmuseum.nl

The headquarters of the Dutch railways is based in Utrecht, so it is fitting that the town has a superb railway museum. Inside, there are modern rail accessories. Outside, visitors can explore steam engines, carriages, trams and signal boxes in five railway "worlds", each with its own theme. Using costumed actors, the museum's "Dream Journeys" experience recreates a journey on the legendary Orient Express from Paris to Constantinople. It summons up the glamour and romance of the golden age of steam.

EAT

Meneer Smakers
Bright and friendly canal-side restaurant serving artisan burgers.

🏛 Nobelstraat 143
🌐 smakers.nl

PALEIS HET LOO

🏠 85 km (53 miles) SE of Amsterdam; Koninklijk Park 1, Apeldoorn
🚆 Apeldoorn, then bus 10, 102 🕐 Gardens & stables: Apr-Sep: 10am-5pm Tue-Sun; Palace: closed for renovation 🌐 paleishetloo.nl

Regarded as the "Versailles of the Netherlands", the palace's Classical façade belies the opulence of its lavish interior. Don't miss the formal gardens and the collection of vintage cars in the stable.

King William III of England, Stadholder of the Netherlands, built Het Loo in 1686 as a royal hunting lodge. Generations of the House of Orange used the lodge as a summer palace. The main architect was Jacob Roman (1640–1716), but the interior decoration and layout of the gardens were the responsibility of Daniel Marot (1661–1752). After extensive restoration work in 1984, Paleis Het Loo opened as a museum. The palace is closed for renovation until mid-2021, but the gardens and stables remain open.

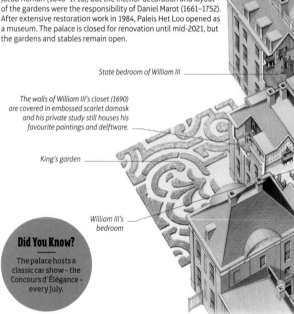

State bedroom of William III

The walls of William III's closet (1690) are covered in embossed scarlet damask and his private study still houses his favourite paintings and delftware.

King's garden

William III's bedroom

Did You Know?

The palace hosts a classic car show - the Concours d'Élégance - every July.

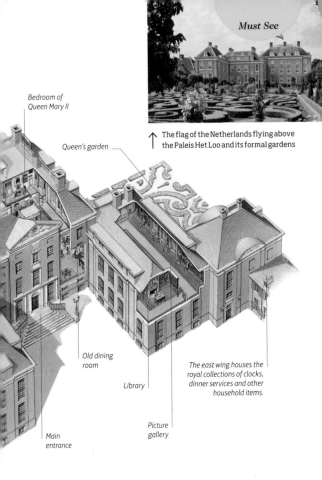

Bedroom of
Queen Mary II

Queen's garden

↑ The flag of the Netherlands flying above
the Paleis Het Loo and its formal gardens

Old dining
room

Library

The east wing houses the
royal collections of clocks,
dinner services and other
household items.

Main
entrance

Picture
gallery

↑ The magnificent Paleis Het Loo,
with its beautiful gardens

Must See

BEFORE YOU GO

Forward planning is essential to any successful trip. Be prepared for all eventualities by considering the following points before you travel.

AT A GLANCE

CURRENCY
Euro (EUR)

AVERAGE DAILY SPEND

SAVE
€80

SPEND
€175

SPLURGE
€250+

Bottled Water
€2.00

Coffee
€3.00

Beer
€5.00

Dinner for Two
€75

ESSENTIAL PHRASES

Hello	Hallo
Goodbye	Dag
Please	Alstublieft
Thank you	Dank u
I'm sorry	Sorry
I don't understand	Ik snap het niet

ELECTRICITY SUPPLY

Power sockets are type C and F, fitting two-pronged plugs. Standard voltage is 230 volts.

Passports and Visas

For stays of up to three months for the purpose of tourism, EU nationals and citizens of the UK, US, Canada, Australia and New Zealand do not need a visa. For visa information specific to your home country, consult your nearest Netherlands embassy or check online.
Netherlands and You
🆆 netherlandsandyou.nl

Travel Safety Advice

Visitors can get up-to-date travel safety information from the **UK Foreign and Commonwealth Office**, the **US State Department** and the **Australian Department of Foreign Affairs and Trade**.
AUS 🆆 smartraveller.gov.au
UK 🆆 gov.uk/foreign-travel-advice
US 🆆 travel.state.gov

Customs Information

An individual is permitted to carry the following within the EU for personal use:
Tobacco products 800 cigarettes, 400 cigarillos, 200 cigars or 1 kg of smoking tobacco.
Alcohol 10 litres of alcoholic beverages above 22% strength, 20 litres of alcoholic beverages below 22% strength, 90 litres of wine (60 litres of which can be sparkling wine) and 110 litres of beer.
Cash If you plan to enter or leave the EU with €10,000 or more in cash (or the equivalent in other currencies) you must declare it to the customs authorities.
If travelling outside the EU limits vary. It is always best to check the restrictions of your home country or next destination before your departure.

Plant and flower bulbs bought in Amsterdam must have a certificate of inspection from the Plant Protection Service if being taken to the USA or Canada.

Insurance

It is wise to take out an insurance policy covering theft, loss of belongings, medical problems, cancellation and delays.

EU and Australian citizens are eligible for discounted or free emergency medical care in the Netherlands. EU citizens should have an **EHIC** (European Health Insurance Card) and Australians should be registered to **Medicare**.

Visitors from outside these areas must arrange their own private medical insurance.

EHIC
W gov.uk/european-health-insurance-card
Medicare
W humanservices.gov.au/individuals/medicare

Vaccinations

No inoculations are needed for the Netherlands.

Money

Most establishments accept major credit, debit and prepaid currency cards, but it's always a good idea to carry some cash, just in case. Contactless payments are widely accepted.

Booking Accommodation

Amsterdam offers a huge variety of accommodation, comprising luxury five-star hotels, family-run B&Bs, budget hostels and even canal houseboat rentals. During peak season lodgings fill up and prices become inflated, so book in advance. A list of accommodation to suit all needs can be found on the **I amsterdam** website.

Travellers with Specific Needs

Despite its winding canals and cobbled streets, Amsterdam is a surprisingly accessible city.

Assistance at **Schiphol Airport** is available free of charge, but must be booked at the same time as your flight.

Accessible Travel Netherlands reviews the accessibility and user-friendliness of restaurants, shops, transport and public buildings in the city.

Main train stations have tactile guidance lines and mobile ramps, and a carer or companion can travel for free through the **NS Travel Assistance** service. Many trains have wheelchair access doors, and most double-decker trains have wheelchair-accessible toilets.

All main pedestrian crossings have sound alerts for the visually impaired.

Accessible Travel Netherlands
W accessibletravelnl.com
NS Travel Assistance
W ns.nl/en/travel-information/traveling-with-a-functional-disability
Schiphol
W schiphol.nl/en/page/extra-assistance

Language

The Dutch have an excellent level of English, some German, French and usually a few other languages too. In Amsterdam you can easily get by without knowing a word of Dutch, but it's appreciated if you can handle a few niceties in the local language. Asking a local if they speak English can be seen as an insult, the implication being that they are uneducated.

Closures

Mondays Some museums and tourist attractions are closed for the day.
Sundays Some shops close early.
Public holidays Schools, post offices, banks and some shops are closed for the entire day; many museums and attractions close early.

GETTING AROUND

Amsterdam is known for its excellent public transport system. However, by far the most enjoyable way to explore this vibrant city is on two wheels.

AT A GLANCE

PUBLIC TRANSPORT COSTS
Tickets are valid on all forms of public transport in Amsterdam.

SINGLE

€3.20
Valid for 1 hour, transfers included

DAY PASS

€8.00
Unlimited travel, day or night

3-DAY PASS

€19.00
Unlimited travel, day or night

SPEED LIMIT

MOTORWAY	DUAL CARRIAGEWAYS
130 km/h (80 mph)	**100** km/h (60 mph)

NATIONAL ROADS	URBAN AREAS
80 km/h (50 mph)	**50** km/h (30 mph)

Arriving by Air

Amsterdam's Schiphol airport is a major international transport hub for destinations around the globe. Schiphol is extremely well connected to Amsterdam city centre by train, bus and taxi. Car rental facilities are also available, although driving in Amsterdam is not recommended. For journey times between the airport and city centre, see the table opposite.

Schiphol Travel Taxi is a shared taxi service that can be booked online as either a private or, for a lower fare, shared taxi. A shared fare starts at around €24 for a single trip, and €42 for a return. A shared taxi may take a longer time than expected, as it can make several stops before your destination.

Connexxion Schiphol Hotel Shuttle is a privately run minibus service that will transport you to and from your hotel. Rates vary depending on how far your hotel is from the airport. Discounts are available for group and family bookings.

Connexxion Schiphol Hotel Shuttle
W schipholhotelshuttle.nl
Schiphol Travel Taxi
W schipholtraveltaxi.nl

Train Travel

International Train Travel
Regular high-speed international trains connect Amsterdam's Centraal Station to other major cities across Europe. Reservations for these services are essential.

You can buy tickets and passes for multiple international journeys from **Eurail** or **Interrail**, however you may still need to pay an additional reservation fee depending on what rail service you travel with. Always check that your pass is valid on the service on which you wish to travel before boarding, as you may be fined for travelling without the correct ticket.

Eurostar runs a reliable and regular service from London to Amsterdam via the Channel Tunnel. However, for the return journey you may need to change in Brussels.

Thalys runs a high-speed rail service between Paris, Brussels and Amsterdam ten times a day. Look out for the variety of special offers, package deals and half-price last-minute deals that the company offers.

NS International also runs a high-speed service between Brussels, Antwerp, Breda, Rotterdam and Amsterdam.

Students and passengers under the age of 26 can benefit from discounted rail travel. For more information on youth fares visit the **Eurail** or **Interrail** website.

Eurail W eurail.com
Eurostar W eurostar.com
Interrail W interrail.eu
NS International W nshispeed.nl
Thalys W thalys.com

Domestic Train Travel

Dutch railways are operated by Nederlandse Spoorwegen (**NS**). The NS Service Centre is located in the western hall of Centraal Station, and provides information on all rail journeys, including live updates and information on delays and changes in schedule. For venturing further afield, the NS offers a wide range of day trips to a variety of locations across the country. Tickets often include a lunch coupon and reduced entry to many Amsterdam museums and attractions. Tickets can be bought online, or from the yellow machines at the front and back entrances of Centraal Station.

NS W ns.nl/en

Public Transport

Centraal Station is the hub for Amsterdam's integrated public transport system (**GVB**).

9292 provides information on all public transport in the city and rest of Netherlands, but it does not make reservations.

9292 W 9292.nl/en
GVB W en.gvb.nl

Tickets

To travel on the metro, trams and buses you will need an OV-chipkaart. There are two kinds: a disposable card valid for either one hour or one to seven days, and a reloadable pass. Both can be bought and topped up at ticket vending machines at stations, GVB ticket offices, some supermarkets and newsagents operating as OV-chipkaart sales points. Avoid buying your OV-chipkaart at Centraal Station, where queues can be very long.

To validate a journey, hold the OV-chipkaart in front of the grey card readers on entering and leaving a metro or train station, or when getting on and off trams and buses. Don't forget to tap it as you disembark or exit – you will be charged more for your journey if you don't.

On all forms of transport, you will be charged the same distance fee, so no one form of transport is cheaper than another.

Children under 4 travel for free on all forms of public transport. Discounted personalized OV-chipkaarten for seniors and 4–11 year olds can be purchased at a GVB office.

Do bear in mind that Amsterdam's city centre is compact, and most of the major sights and shopping areas are within close walking distance from one another. You will save money and see more of the city on foot.

Buses

The majority of Amsterdam's buses depart from Centraal Station, branching out from the city centre with the same stops as the trams.

Bus 22 connects the centre to the eastern and western parts of the city. Take this bus to visit Jordaan and the Western Islands.

Night buses, numbered 281 to 293, run all night, with services every hour during the week and every half hour at weekends. Fares start at €4.50 per ride.

Long-Distance Bus Travel

Long-distance bus or coach travel can be a cheap option for travellers. **National Express** and **Flixbus** offer a variety of routes to Amsterdam from other European cities. Fares start from £22, with discounts for students and children.

Flixbus 🚐 flixbus.co.uk
National Express 🚐 nationalexpress.com

Trams

The most useful routes go south from Centraal Station along Damrak or Nieuwezijds Voorburgwal (2, 4, 11, 12, 13, 14, 17, 24), diverging after the Singel. Lines 13 and 17 are also useful if you need to travel west into Jordaan.

Trams operate from 6am on weekdays and 7am at weekends, finishing just after midnight, when night buses take over.

Metro

Amsterdam's underground system comprises five lines, three of which start from and terminate at Centraal Station. There are seven stations in the centre. From Amsterdam CS (Centraal Station) you either take the eastern line (51, 53, 54), stopping at Nieuwmarkt, Waterlooplein and Weesperplein, or you can hop on the Noord/Zuidlijn (52) to travel to Rokin, Vijzelgracht and De Pijp.

Taxis

Official taxis have a blue numberplate and display their registration number on the windscreen. They should always run a meter. Taxis are not hailed, but picked up at official taxi stands (*kwaliteitstaxistandplaatsen*) situated at main stations and squares or close to key tourist sights. Taxi apps such as Uber also operate in Amsterdam. The following services can be booked by phone or online:

Amsterdam Taxi Online 🚕 amsterdamtaxi-online.com
Sneltaxi 🚕 sneltaxi.nl
TCA Taxicentrale 🚕 tcataxi.nl/en.html

Driving

Driving in Amsterdam is not recommended. Small inner-city streets, canals, parking shortages and complicated one-way systems all make Amsterdam ill-suited to getting around by car. Public transport is a much more efficient way of travelling around the city.

Driving to Amsterdam

The Netherlands is easily reached by car from most European countries via E-roads, the International European Road Network. Major roads (N roads) and motorways (A roads) are well maintained. From the A10 ring road, the S-routes (marked by blue signs) will take you to the centre of Amsterdam. To take your own car into the Netherlands, you will need proof of registration, valid insurance documents, a road safety certificate from the vehicle's country of origin and an international identification disc. Vehicles may also be transported into the country by international ferry or rail.

Car Rental

To rent a car in the Netherlands you must be 19 or over and have held a valid driver's licence for at least a year. EU driving licences issued by any of the EU member states are valid throughout the European Union. If visiting from outside the EU, you may need to apply for an International Driving Permit (IDP). Check with your local automobile association before you travel.

Driving in Amsterdam

If you do decide to take to the roads in Amsterdam, it is important to be aware of the many one-way systems in place in the city centre. When driving in the canal area, remember that the water should be to your left. Park-and-ride facilities, available on the outskirts of the city, are much cheaper and less stressful than parking in the city centre. The **ANWB** (the Royal Dutch Touring Club) provides a breakdown service for

members of foreign motoring organizations. A non-member can pay for the ANWB's services, or become a temporary ANWB member for the duration of their stay.
ANWB Ⓦ anwb.nl

Rules of the Road

Drive on the right. Unless otherwise signposted, vehicles coming from the right have right of way. Passing or turning is forbidden on roads with a continuous white line. At all times, drivers must carry a valid driver's licence, registration and insurance documents. The wearing of seat belts is compulsory, and the use of a mobile phone while driving is prohibited, with the exception of a hands-free system. Headlights should be dipped in built-up areas. It is prohibited to use sidelights only. The Dutch strictly enforce speed limits on their roads, and use traffic enforcement cameras in urban areas and radar guns on national roads and motorways. The Netherlands strictly enforces its drink-drive limit.

Cycling

By far the best way to get around Amsterdam is by bicycle. The city's traffic system favours cyclists. There is also an excellent network of cycle lanes (*fietspaden*), dedicated traffic lights and road signs, as well as special routes linking up different parts of the city. There are many bike parking facilities conveniently placed around the city, usually near main stations and busy squares. Bicycle theft in Amsterdam is rife. Always secure your bike even when parking for just a few minutes to deter potential bike thieves. Hire shops are happy to advise on security matters, and a bike lock will normally be included in the rental price.

Bicycle Hire

Rental costs start at around €10 per day for a basic, single-gear, back-pedal brake bike. Since Amsterdam is so flat, gears are not essential. Bikes with gears and other add-ons will be more expensive.

Deposits are usually paid upfront and refunded on return. You may have to leave your passport or ID for the duration of the rental. **MacBike** and **Orange Bike** offer optional extras such as children's seats, paniers, saddlebags and rain gear.
MacBike Ⓦ macbike.nl
Orange Bike Ⓦ orange-bike.nl

Bicycle Safety

Ride on the right. If you are unsure or unsteady, practise in one of the inner city parks first.

If in doubt, dismount: many novices cross busy junctions on foot; if you do so, switch to the pedestrian section of the crossing. Beware of tram tracks; cross them at an angle to avoid getting stuck.

Do not walk with your bike in a bike lane or cycle on pavements, on the left side of the road, in pedestrian zones, or at night without lights. If caught doing so you will face a hefty fine. The locals usually don't bother, but it is a wise precaution to wear a helmet, particularly if you are planning on cycling on the roads.

Bicycle Tours

Guided bicycle tours are a popular way to discover the city and its environs. The following offer popular tours:
Joy Ride Tours Ⓦ joyridetours.nl
Mikes Bike Tours Ⓦ mikesbiketours amsterdam.com
Yellowbike Tours and Rental Ⓦ yellowbike.nl

Boats and Ferries

The Dutchflyer is a rail and sail service that runs from London to Amsterdam via Harwich and the Hook of Holland. **P&O Ferries** operates an overnight service from Hull to Zeebrugge or Rotterdam where you can transfer to Amsterdam's Centraal Station.
The Dutchflyer Ⓦ stenaline.co.uk/ferry-to-holland/rail-and-sail
P&O Ferries Ⓦ poferries.com/en/portal

PRACTICAL INFORMATION

A little local know-how goes a long way in Amsterdam. Here you will find all the essential advice and information you will need during your stay.

EMERGENCY NUMBERS

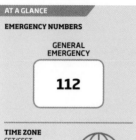

GENERAL
EMERGENCY

112

TIME ZONE

CET/CEST
Central European
Summer Time
(CEST) runs end
Mar–end Oct

TAP WATER

Tap water in the
Netherlands is
safe to drink.

TIPPING

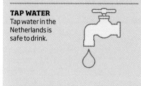

Waiter	5–10%
Hotel Porter	€1 a bag
Housekeeping	€1 a day
Concierge	€1–2
Taxi Driver	Not expected

Personal Security

Pickpockets work crowded tourist areas, trams and trains between the city centre and Schiphol airport. Be alert to your surroundings.

If you have anything stolen, report the crime as soon as possible to the nearest police station.

Bring ID with you and get a copy of the crime report in order to claim on your insurance.

Bar and club areas like Leidseplein and Rembrandtplein, the Red Light District and city parks can be dangerous for lone tourists in the early hours.

If you have your passport stolen, or in the event of a serious crime, contact your consulate in Amsterdam, or your embassy in Den Haag.

Health

Minor ailments can be dealt with by a chemist *(drogist)*. For prescriptions go to a pharmacy *(apotheek)*. Details of the nearest 24-hour service are posted in all pharmacy windows.

The **Central Medical Service** *(Centrale Doktersdienst)* will direct you to the nearest pharmacy, and can refer you to a GP or dentist. EU citizens can receive emergency medical and dental treatment in the Netherlands at a reduced charge. You may have to pay upfront for medical treatment and reclaim on your insurance later.

Visitors from outside the EU or Australia are responsible for the payment of hospital and other medical expenses. As such it is important to arrange comprehensive medical insurance.

Central Medical Service
w doktersdienst.info

Smoking, Alcohol and Drugs

The Netherlands has a smoking ban in all public places, including bars, restaurants, cafés and hotels. Confusingly, this also applies to coffee shops, where smoking cannabis is decriminalized, but smoking tobacco is illegal. Foreign tourists were banned from entering coffee shops in 2013, although Amsterdam police tend to turn a blind eye to this. Soft drugs such as hashish and cannabis are decriminalized for personal use. Hard drugs are a different matter: any-one caught with them by the police will certainly be prosecuted. Never try to take drugs out of the Netherlands: if caught you will face prosecution. Alcohol consumption is illegal in parks, and on the streets in nightlife areas such as Leidseplein, Rembrandtplein and the Red Light District. The Netherlands has a strict limit of 0.05% BAC (blood alcohol content) for drivers and cyclists.

ID

In the Netherlands, everyone over the age of 14 is legally required to carry ID, including tourists. You can be fined for not having the correct ID, so carry your passport, or a photo-copy of your passport, with you at all times.

Local Customs

Do not photograph prostitutes in the Red Light District – this will anger local sex workers. Avoid using cameras and recording equipment in the area, as someone may mistake your intentions.

Visiting Churches and Cathedrals

Dress respectfully: cover your torso and upper arms; ensure shorts and skirts cover your knees.

Mobile Phones and Wi-Fi

Free Wi-Fi hot spots are widely available in Amsterdam's city centre. Cafés and restaurants usually permit the use of their Wi-Fi on the condition that you make a purchase. Visitors travelling to Amsterdam with EU mobile phone tariffs won't be affected by data roaming charges. Users will be charged the same rates for data, SMS and voice calls as they would pay at home.

Post

Stamps (*postzegels*) can be bought in shops, supermarkets, newsagents or tobacconists. Send items of value by registered mail from the post office (*postagentschap*).

Taxes and Refunds

VAT is 21% in the Netherlands. Non-EU residents are entitled to a tax refund subject to certain conditions. Shops that stock the relevant forms will have a sign saying "Tax free for tourists". When leaving the country, present this form at customs, along with the goods receipt and your ID, to receive your refund.

Discount Cards

The following discount cards are available to tourists for a set fee. It is wise to consider carefully how many of the offers you are likely to take advantage of before purchasing, as they can be expensive.

I amsterdam City Card Includes unlimited travel on public transport, a canal tour and free or discounted access to most museums and attractions. Available online and from all tourist offices. Valid for either 24 (€60), 48 (€80), 72 (€95) or 120 (€115) hours.

Museum Card (Museumkaart) Offers discounted admission to over 400 museums in the Netherlands for one year. Available from tourist offices, online and at museums for €64.90 (adults) and €32.45 (under-25s).

CJP Card Under-30s can enjoy discounts on museums, festivals, fashion and more. Available online and from tourist offices.

INDEX

ACKNOWLEDGMENTS

Dorling Kindersley would like to extend special thanks to the following people for their contribution: Syed Mohammad Farhan, Narender Kumar, Shanker Prasad, Bandana Paul, Vaishali Vashisht, Tanveer Zaidi.

The publisher would like to thank the following for their kind permission to reproduce their photographs:

Key: a-above; b-below/bottom; c-centre; f-far; l-left; r-right; t-top

123RF.com: Nattee Chalermtiragool 12bl; ekinyalgin 74t; NEMO by Renzo Piano Building Workshop, architects / Markus Gann 29b; macfromlondon 40-1b; mediagram 47tl; William Perry 37r; phototraveller 12cl.

500px: Bart van Dijk 70b.

A'DAM Toren: 81bl.

Alamy Stock Photo: Dutch Cities 93tl; eye35.pix 20b; Chris Harris 3tl; hemis.fr / René Mattes 82b; imageBROKER / Alexander Pöschel 68br./ Carlos Sanchez 66b; Frans Lemmens 86, 88clb; Daryl Mulvihill 69tr; Mo Peerbacus 63tr; StockphotoVideo 11crb.

Amsterdam Museum: 7crb; Portrait Gallery of the Golden Age, Hermitage Museum 76b;

Caro Bonink 7t.

Anne Frank House: Cris Toala Olivares 35tr.

AWL Images: Francesco Riccardo Iacomin 84b.

De Nieuwe Kerk: Erik en Petra Hesmerg 8bl.

Dreamstime.com: Andreykr 46-7b; Mihai Andritoiu 6b; Antonfrolov 23tl; Artur Bogacki 26tl, 79cra; Boris Breytman 53l; Devy 89tr; Digikhmer 14tl; Serban Enache 56b; Inna Felker 30bl; Harmen Goedhart 44b; Peter Hoeks 55br; Pavel Kavalenkau 51tr; Jan Kranendonk 9crb; Mihai-bogdan Lazar 19crb; Ethan Le 80b; Mastroraf 92bl; Martin Molcan 62b; TasFoto 90clb; Alexander Tolstykh 45t; Tomas1111 16b, 39t; Tonyv3112 38bl; Tupungato 61br; VanderWolfImages 94t; Dennis Van De Water 48cra, 50br.

Foam Museum: Foam Talent 2016, Mercatorplein 58br.

Getty Images: AFP / Lex Van Lieshout 97tr; Atlantide Phototravel 34b.

Hash Marihuana & Hemp Museum Amsterdam / Barcelona: 32clb.

IJ Hallen: Nichon Glerum 83tr.

iStockphoto.com: ahavelaar 27br; Deejpilot 60-1t;

Aleksandar Georgiev 2t; JacobH 99tr; justhavealook 10bl; KavalenkavaVolha 64clb; mila103 22clb; narvikk 4-5b; pidjoe 15bc, 43crb, 71t; Siempreverde22 87crb; TasfotoNL 96b.

Joods Historisch Museum: Liselore Kamping 25crb; Marijke Volkers 24clb.

Museum Het Rembrandthuis: 21tl, 21tr.

National Maritime Museum Amsterdam (Het Scheepvaartmuseum): Twycer 71cra.

Oude Kerk, Amsterdam: GJ Van Rooij 23tr.

Stedelijk Museum: Marc Chagall / Chagall ® / © ADAGP, Paris and DACS, London 2018 Le violoniste (The Fiddler), 1912-13 on loan from the Cultural Heritage Agency 48bl; Gert Jan van Rooij 49.

Rijksmuseum van Oudheden: Mike Bink 91tr.

SuperStock: Mauritius / Ernst Wrba 67tl.

Tropenmuseum: Collectie Stichting Nationaal Museum van Wereldculturen. Coll.nr. TM-2357-77 73bl; Rob van Esch 72; Jakob van Vliet 73cra.

Verzetsmuseum: 77tr.

For further information see: www.dkimages.com

PHRASE BOOK

IN EMERGENCY

Help!	**Help!**	*Help*
Stop!	**Stop!**	*Stop*
Call a doctor	**Haal een dokter**	*Haal uhn* **dok**-*tur*
Call an ambulance	**Bel een ambulance**	*Bell uhn ahm-bew-***luhns**-*uh*
Call the police	**Roep de politie**	*Roop duh poe-***leet**-*see*
Call the fire brigade	**Roep de brandweer**	*Roop duh* **brahnt**-*vheer*
Where is the nearest telephone?	**Waar is de dichtstbijzijnde telefoon?**	*Vhaar iss duh* **dikhst**-*baiy-zaiyn-duh tay-luh-***foan**
Where is the nearest hospital?	**Waar is het dichtstbijzijnde ziekenhuis?**	*Vhaar iss het* **dikhst**-*baiy-zaiyn-duh* **zee**-*kuh-houws*

COMMUNICATION ESSENTIALS

Yes	**Ja**	*Yaa*
No	**Nee**	*Nay*
Please	**Alstublieft**	*Ahls-tew-***bleeft**
Thank you	**Dank u**	*Dahnk-ew*
Excuse me	**Pardon**	*Pahr-***don**
Hello	**Hallo**	*Hallo*
Goodbye	**Dag**	*Dahgh*
Good night	**Slaap lekker**	*Slaap* **lek**-*kah*
morning	**Morgen**	**Mor**-*ghuh*
afternoon	**Middag**	**Mid**-*dahgh*
evening	**Avond**	**Ah**-*vohnd*
yesterday	**Gisteren**	**Ghis**-*tern*
today	**Vandaag**	*Vahn-***daagh**
tomorrow	**Morgen**	**Mor**-*ghuh*
here	**Hier**	*Heer*
there	**Daar**	*Daar*
What?	**Wat?**	*Vhat*
When?	**Wanneer?**	*Vhan-***eer**
Why?	**Waarom?**	*Vhaar-***om**
Where?	**Waar?**	*Vhaar*
How?	**Hoe?**	*Hoo*

USEFUL PHRASES

How are you?	**Hoe gaat het ermee?**	*Hoo ghaat het er-***may**
Very well, thank you	**Heel goed, dank u**	*Hayl ghoot, dahnk ew*
How do you do?	**Hoe maakt u het?**	*Hoo maakt ew het*
See you soon	**Tot ziens**	*Tot zeens*
That's fine	**Prima**	**Pree**-*mah*
Where is/are?	**Waar is/zijn?**	*Vhaar iss/zayn*
How far is it to...?	**Hoe ver is het naar...?**	*Hoo vehr iss het naar...*
How do I get to ...?	**Hoe kom ik naar...?**	*Hoo kom ik naar...*
Do you speak English?	**Spreekt u engels?**	*Spraykt ew* **eng**-*uhls*
I don't understand	**Ik snap het niet**	*Ik snahp het neet*
Could you speak slowly?	**Kunt u langzamer praten?**	*Kuhnt ew* **lahng**-*zahmer praa-tuh*
I'm sorry	**Sorry**	*Sorry*

USEFUL WORDS

big	**groot**	*ghroaht*
small	**klein**	*klaiyn*
hot	**warm**	*vharm*
cold	**koud**	*khowt*
good	**goed**	*ghoot*
bad	**slecht**	*slekht*
enough	**genoeg**	*ghuh-***noohkh**
well	**goed**	*ghoot*
open	**open**	*open*
closed	**gesloten**	*ghuh-***slow**-*tuh*
left	**links**	*links*
right	**rechts**	*rekhts*
straight on	**rechtdoor**	*rehkht dohr*
near	**dichtbij**	*dikht baiy*
far	**ver weg**	*vehr vhekh*
up	**omhoog**	*om-***hoakh**
down	**naar beneden**	*naar buh-***nay**-*duh*

English	Dutch	Pronunciation
early	**vroeg**	*vroohkh*
late	**laat**	*laat*
entrance	**ingang**	*in-ghahng*
exit	**uitgang**	*ouht-ghang*
toilet	**wc**	*vhay say*
occupied	**bezet**	*buh-**zett***
free (unoccupied)	**vrij**	*vraiy*
free (no charge)	**gratis**	**ghraah**-*tiss*

SHOPPING

How much does this cost?	**Hoeveel kost dit?**	*Hoo-**vayl** kost dit*
I would like	**Ik wil graag**	*Ik vhil ghraakh*
Do you have...?	**Heeft u...?**	*Hayft ew...*
I'm just looking	**Ik kijk alleen even**	*Ik kaiyk alleyn **ay**-vuh*
Do you take credit cards?	**Neemt u credit cards aan?**	*Naymt ew credit cards aan*
Do you take travellers' cheques?	**Neemt u reischeques aan?**	*Naymt ew **raiys**-sheks aan*
What time do you open?	**Hoe laat gaat u open?**	*Hoo laat ghaat ew opuh*
What time do you close?	**Hoe laat gaat u dicht?**	*Hoo laat ghaat ew dikht*
This one	**Deze**	*Day-zuh*
That one	**Die**	*Dee*
expensive	**duur**	*dewr*
cheap	**goedkoop**	*ghoot-**koap***
size	**maat**	*maat*
white	**wit**	*vhit*
black	**zwart**	*zvhahrt*
red	**rood**	*roat*
yellow	**geel**	*ghayl*
green	**groen**	*ghroon*
blue	**blauw**	*blah-ew*

SIGHTSEEING

art gallery	**galerie**	*ghaller-ee*
bus station	**busstation**	**buhs**-*stah-shown*
cathedral	**kathedraal**	*kah-tuh-**draal***
church	**kerk**	*kehrk*
closed on public holidays	**op feestdagen gesloten**	*op **fayst**-daa-ghuh ghuh-**slow**-tuh*
day return	**dagretour**	*dahgh-ruh-tour*
garden	**tuin**	*touwn*
library	**bibliotheek**	*bee-bee-yo-**tayk***
museum	**museum**	*mew-**zay**-uhm*
railway station	**station**	*stah-**shown***
return ticket	**retourtje**	*ruh-**tour**-tyuh*
single journey	**enkeltje**	**eng**-*kuhl-tyuh*
tourist information	**VVV**	*fay fay fay*
town hall	**stadhuis**	*staht-**houws***
train	**trein**	*tr.aiyn*
travel pass	**Ov-chipkaart**	*oh-**vay**-chip-kaahrt*

EATING OUT

Have you got a table?	**Is er een tafel vrij?**	*Iss ehr uhn **tah**-fuhl vraiy*
I want to reserve a table	**Ik wil een tafel reserveren**	*Ik vhil uhn **tah**-fuhl ray-sehr-**veer**-uh*
The bill, please	**Mag ik afrekenen**	*Mukh ik **ahf**-ray-kuh-nuh*
I am a vegetarian	**Ik ben vegetariër**	*Ik ben fay-ghuh-**taahr**-ee-er*
waitress/waiter	**serveerster/ober**	*Sehr-**veer**-ster/oh-ber*
menu	**de kaart**	*duh kaahrt*
cover charge	**het couvert**	*het koo-**vehr***
wine list	**de wijnkaart**	*duh **vhaiyn**-kaart*
breakfast	**het ontbijt**	*het ont-**baiyt***
lunch	**de lunch**	*duh lernsh*
dinner	**het diner**	*het dee-**nay***
bar	**het cafe**	*het kaa-**fay***
café	**het eetcafe**	*het **ayt**-kaa-fay*
rare	**rare**	*rare*
medium	**medium**	*medium*
well done	**doorbakken**	*dohr-**bah**-kuh*

NUMBERS

1	**een**	*ayn*
2	**twee**	*tvhay*
3	**drie**	*dree*
4	**vier**	*feer*
5	**vijf**	*faiyf*
6	**zes**	*zess*
7	**zeven**	**zay**-*vuh*
8	**acht**	*ahkht*
9	**negen**	**nay**-*guh*
10	**tien**	*teen*
11	**elf**	*elf*
12	**twaalf**	*tvhaalf*
13	**dertien**	**dehr**-*teen*
14	**veertien**	**feer**-*teen*
15	**vijftien**	**faiyf**-*teen*
16	**zestien**	**zess**-*teen*
17	**zeventien**	**zayvuh**-*teen*
18	**achttien**	**ahkh**-*teen*
19	**negentien**	**nay**-*ghuh-teen*
20	**twintig**	**tvhin**-*tukh*
21	**eenentwintig**	**aynuh**-*tvhin-tukh*
30	**dertig**	**dehr**-*tukh*
40	**veertig**	**feer**-*tukh*
50	**vijftig**	**faiyf**-*tukh*
60	**zestig**	**zess**-*tukh*
70	**zeventig**	**zay**-*vuh-tukh*
80	**tachtig**	**tahkh**-*tukh*
90	**negentig**	**nayguh**-*tukh*
100	**honderd**	**hohn**-*durt*
1000	**duizend**	**douw**-*zuhnt*
1,000,000	**miljoen**	*mill-**yoon***

TIME

one minute	**een minuut**	*uhn meen-ewt*
one hour	**een uur**	*uhn ewr*
half an hour	**een half uur**	*uhn hahlf ewr*
half past one	**half twee**	*hahlf tvhay*
a day	**een dag**	*uhn dahgh*
a week	**een week**	*uhn vhayk*
a month	**een maand**	*uhn maant*
a year	**een jaar**	*uhn jaar*
Monday	**maandag**	**maan**-*dahgh*
Tuesday	**dinsdag**	**dins**-*dahgh*
Wednesday	**woensdag**	**vhoons**-*dahgh*
Thursday	**donderdag**	**donder**-*dahgh*
Friday	**vrijdag**	**vraiy**-*dahgh*
Saturday	**zaterdag**	**zaater**-*dahgh*
Sunday	**zondag**	**zon**-*dahgh*